Wrestling To Rasslin

Wrestling To Rasslin:
Ancient Sport to American Spectacle

Gerald W. Morton
George M. O'Brien

Bowling Green State University Popular Press
Bowling Green, Ohio 43403

Library of Congress Catalogue Card No.: 85-70425

ISBN: 0-87972-323-8 Clothbound
        0-87972-324-6 Paperback

Contents

Foreword

Gerald W. Morton
George M. O'Brien

Speculations about which is the oldest sport reach stalemate when the list is reduced by logic to running, wrestling and lifting. We argue that wrestling deserves the distinction as the first sport. Superficially, running seems the obvious choice for the oldest sport. But prehistoric runners, like millions of joggers today, could have been lone competitors striving against self or terrain rather than participants playing together. Wrestling, on the other hand, is social by its very nature and to exist requires the other, friend or foe. Wrestling, then, is always contest regardless of whether engaged in as mere play or struggle. Lifting and tossing events claim primacy because they, too, are instinctive exercises; but the need for an instrument such as rock or javelin seems to put them a moment in time beyond the basic body chess of wrestling.

An even more fruitless debate can occur when the issue of the modern professional wrestling match is broached. All meaningful discourse eventually falters in the face of the disclaimer, "but it isn't real." Translated "but it isn't sport," this evaluation is accurate, if one defines, as we did above, sport as contest. Wrestling, however, is certainly real as a quick turn of the television dial on Saturday afternoon will testify. The issue should, therefore, be what is this phenomenon professional wrestling and why has its popularity become such that in 1985 more people will attend a professional wrestling match than will witness a professional baseball game.

The first chapter of this study pieces together the mosaic of wrestling starting with the earliest records. Styles from various cultures are cited to help fill out the historical picture.

1

Finally the development of the game in the United States is traced from colonial times through the rise in the nineteenth century of amateur and professional sport and concludes with conditions during the Depression years.

Chapter Two examines professional wrestling in the era of television. It is studied as a business dependent upon media and fans for survival and profit. The new spectacle entertainment is examined in its structure and organization; attention is given to the people on the inside who keep it alive.

The third chapter deals with the parallels between professional wrestling and the various theatrical traditions from which it draws. What is vital is that the reader see that these similarities are not accidental but rather an inherent part of the orchestration of the game.

Chapter four examines the participants in the wrestling drama, particularly those characteristics of a wrestler's persona which make him a hero or villain. Especial attention is given to pointing out types of heroes and villains and discussing why these types are employed.

The final chapter discusses wrestling as ritual. Because wrestling is neither completely drama nor completely sport, we feel that the label of ritual is justified as we examine the game, measuring it against the characteristics which sociologists have outlined for ritual activity.

The material in this book is generally descriptive rather than critical. Our concern has been to provide a foundation on which future discussions of professional wrestling can rest solidly. Ours is not, therefore, a definitive study, nor was it intended to be. Rather, we hope that the work will finally draw attention to this very interesting manifestation of popular culture and motivate critical research into its nature.

Chapter One
Demise and Rebirth:
The Cyclic History of Wrestling

Wrestlers are a sluggish set, and of dubious health. They sleep out their lives, and whenever they depart ever so little from their regular diet they fall seriously ill.

Plato, *Republic*, III

The fascinating, colorful annals of wrestling, the oldest prole sport, are reduced to a few dull, dead paragraphs in standard reference works. No recent reliable history of the sport exists. Wrestling, as common sense tells us and as reference entries tiredly repeat, is a very ancient sport. In accounts of its history, the catalog of times and places has almost become canonical. First the struggles with beasts and rivals by prehistoric cave-dwellers are dutifully recalled. Next artifacts and pictorial portrayals of wrestling found in Egypt, France and the Near East are described. Then writers expand in glorifying the classic harmony found in a balance between track and field events (read: "true athletics") with wrestling and boxing in the celebrated Greek games of yore. The survival of wrestling as a popular activity is noted despite the rejection of sport as pagan behavior from the early Christian era through the late Middle Ages. At this point in the text the chronicler of wrestling is hard put to fill in a gap of nearly two millenia and so often turns to amusing anecdotes including the "battle royal" between Henry VIII and Francis I. Or the narrative is expanded with sketches of cultures outside the European tradition such as descriptions of sumo in Japan. With the coming of the nineteenth century, modern sport is born. This period brings a new problem that is seldom clearly resolved. How can the dichotomy between amateur and professional wrestling today be explained by the past? The

3

orthodox but distorted solution is to present the amateur sport as an outgrowth of nascent college athletics, muscular Christianity, sporting clubs and the modern Olympic movement with a curious admixture of popular nineteenth-century American sport. Professional wrestling is conveniently traced to popular origins in post Civil War America. But in the unruly gaslit era confusion enters with the advent of promoters, the road or stage circuit, a boisterous paying public, betting and crooked dealing, conflicting claims to championships and titles, and the arrival of wrestlers from abroad. Nostalgia and personal prejudice determine when the writer chooses to date the end of professional wrestling as a sport and its metamorphosis into an exhibition or a show. Frank Gotch retired in 1913, for some as the last pure and true champion; others give that honor to Ed "Strangler" Lewis, as late as 1932. The profitable wedding of wrestling to the new popular medium of television after the second World War definitely marks the end of references to sport in the entries on wrestling. "Pro" wrestling from that point on is called an exhibition, a show, or—in the insider's jargon—"the game." But note the disquieting fact that the Olympics are still called games rather than sports.

Too often the chroniclers of wrestling have been distracted by sand tossed in their eyes and have been thrown for a loss while they debated the bogus argument of whether or not wrestling is a sport. The history of wrestling can be a reputable, legitimate study that provides insight into many aspects of life. A confident yet cautious approach from the stance of popular culture lets the writer feel out the facts before coming to grips with a tough topic that has escaped many an attempt to pin it down. (Yes, wrestling has enriched English with metaphors and cliches.) Wrestling has always been a sport of the people, a prole sport in three regards. First, it has been found as a scheduled activity or impromptu game when common people in many cultures gather on festive occasions. Second, the participants have regularly come from the common folk rather than from the aristocratic classes. And third, the audience it draws is composed predominantly of ordinary people; its appeal is not exclusive or limited to an initiated elite. This chapter traces the story of wrestling as a recurrent popular phenomenon.

The origins of wrestling are lost in prehistory. The fact poses problems—anthropological, biological, sociological, philosophical—which the writer should consider while exercising poetic license. The saga of wrestling, however, deserves to be told despite any possible confusion as to fact and fiction. After all, even the beginnings of such modern sports as baseball engender much controversy. The first question about wrestling arises quite naturally: How far back can the sport be traced? The playful tussling of animals encourages anthropomorphic speculation on the one hand. On the other, even today remnants of prehistoric totemism are found when wrestlers and other athletes assume epithets from the animal kingdom such as bear, gorilla and tiger.

The myriad examples of play including wrestling among animals convinced the philosopher Johan Huizinga that play precedes culture and is not an outgrowth of human society.[1] Thus attempts at explaining the origin and purpose of play fail because they derive from theories of human society and culture which are of later origin. The fun of playing, for example, evades logical categorization and exists in its own right. An ironic line by the French social and sport psychologist Rogert Callois illustrates the absence of human purpose and the work ethic in play. He quipped: "Play is ... an occasion of pure waste: waste of time, energy, ingenuity, skill."[2] There is unresolved paradox in that human beings at play, while displaying animal energy and aptitude, strive to transcend human limits in the arena and on the playing field. Play locales are carefully set aside like religious sanctuaries; activity there is free of mundane purpose and real time.

Still logic suggests that wrestling grew out of the struggles of prehistoric human beings when hunting beasts or when attacked by them. Also, warfare with other tribes and contests within the group for dominance as well as for mates contributed to the development of wrestling holds and escapes. The very universality of wrestling in cultures from all inhabited continents and all eras is evidence that in time wrestling passed from an early stage of pure work to play. Sociologist Gregory Stone notes the significance of the survival of former work forms as play: "An important function of play is the *re*creation and maintenance of obsolete work forms, making history a viable reality for mankind. Thus canoeing, archery, and horseback riding persist in society today as play. Wrestling is no exception."[3]

Play is not used here as a synonym for simple frivolity or pure pastime. Wrestling as play could be and often was a very serious activity indeed. It has been a formal rite prescribed for special occasions such as the funeral games described by Homer, or harvest festivals in ancient Japan, or an activity required of bachelors prior to mating dances among the people of Kau up to our own day.

Evidence of wrestling, an instinctive and natural sport, is also widely found as an activity imposed on youths to develop agility, balance, strength and wit. Together with running, the other instinctual sport, wrestling requires no special equipment or even initial training for participants. For these reasons it was the best example of prole sport in antiquity and has remained so to modern times.

It could also be called the most popular sport until modern times if the numbers and the social classes of those actually wrestling are considered. It was the common man's sport in ancient Egypt and Greece, in medieval England and France and in America among Indians and frontiersmen. In biblical times Jews practised belt wrestling. Vikings of the sagas fostered backhold and *glinna* or belt wrestling as do their descendants in Iceland today. At folk festivals Swiss yeomen still engage in their version of belt wrestling called *Schwingen*. Turks and Iranians wear leather breeches as did their ancestors while Cornish farmers don the simple canvas jacket of their forefathers for wrestling. In all these variants as well as many more, raiment is simple, and elaborate sporting equipment is absent. Wrestling is the commoner's sport. The situation in Japan, though complex, well illustrates the class distinction. The national sport of sumo while now highly ritualized has basically no special equipment and is the ancient form of wrestling dating from a mythic bout in which a Shinto god won the islands from an aborigine champion. Ju-Jitso and karate, while traced in lore back to the same ancient contest, betray aristocratic or samurai development in the prescribed uniforms, hierarchic ranks and martial posturings.

In 1938 while excavating the 5000 year old Sumerian temple of Kyfaje near Baghdad, American anthropologists found two important artifacts. One was a stone relief depicting boxers squaring off; the other was a cast bronze figurine of wrestlers gripping each other's hips or belts. This statuette is the oldest known record of wrestling. It is significant that it was found at a religious site, for historians agree in tracing the origins of wrestling in ancient times to cults celebrating life and death. In Egyptian tombs stone friezes and paintings of wrestlers have been found. The most interesting discovery is the wrestling manual painted on the walls of a temple dating from 1850 B.C. at Beni Hasan halfway up the Nile. Nearly 400 paintings depicting the course of a match show the Egyptians knew most of the holds and escapes practiced in modern freestyle wrestling. Written taunts accompanying the mural suggest the ancients tried to "psyche out" opponents too: "I'm going to pin you.—I'll make you weep in your heart and cringe with fear.—Look, I'm going to make you fall and faint away right in front of the Pharaoh."[4] Well instructed in the art of wrestling, the deceased was prepared to conquer any opponent in the world beyond.

Athletics in classical Greece were diverse and complex. This befits a culture which developed over 1500 years of recorded history and spread outward from a small homeland sung in epic by Homer to the Hellenic world prospering on three continents following the conquests of Alexander. The tale of wrestling in the Greek and later Roman world reflects many facets of this long history. Myth says rules for the sport were established by the Athenian hero and king Theseus who had conquered the murderous Cercyon by skill rather than brute force in a wrestling match. But as is typical in mythology, another version proclaims the goddess Palaestra, daughter of Mercury, the inventor of wrestling. Her name lives on in the building, the palaestra, which was originally an enclosed practice area for wrestling and boxing.

Historically speaking, wrestling originated in Greek ritual long before there were any structures and established rules. In chapter 23 of the *Iliad*, Homer gives the detailed moves in the match between Ajax and Odysseus, which was one event in the funeral games held in honor of Patroclus. Experts have hotly

8   Wrestling To Rasslin

debated whether or not rite in a restricted sense is the origin of
Greek athletics. Some point out the Homeric narratives portray
love of contest and pure impromptu sport rather than serious
activity. More importantly they note that in the Homeric
contests, unlike later games, only nobles were allowed to
compete for the valued prizes. The original funeral games, they
argue, were simply a device for distributing the possessions of
a dead leader. Opposing scholars document over thirty
panhellenic festivals or games traced to funeral rites in honor
of mythic heroes including the Olympics in honor of Pelops
and an equal number of funeral games held to honor historic
personages including those who died at Marathon and several
games called by Alexander who declared them a legitimate
claim of the dead. Perhaps the debate is misfocused. The
Greeks, conservative by nature and free of modern distinctions
between work, play and religion, did establish canons for the
games which reflect many similarities with recognized rites.
Sports, rites and liturgy are all "useless but meaningful," as
Romano Guardini, an expert on liturgy, once noted. Whatever
their origin, Greek athletic festivals right from the beginning
included wrestling as an event.

The games served as a cultural bond along with language,
religion and commerce in an ever expanding Hellenic world.
Norman Gardiner notes that they are remarkable in their
continuity: "The sports of the eighth century B.C. are the same
as those of Homer—the chariot-race, the foot-race, throwing
the diskos and the javelin, wrestling, and boxing. These events
with certain variations and additions make up the programme
of the athletic festivals of Greece during their whole history;
they survive the loss of Greek independence, are taken over by
Rome, and in places are still found even after the fall of the
Roman Empire."[5] While the games continued, they
nonetheless evolved as the development in ancient Greece of
various styles of wrestling demonstrates.

Wrestling in the ancient Olympic, Pythian, Isthmian and
other national and local games was not, as commonly reported,
the same sport as modern Greco-Roman wrestling. During the
1200 year history of the Olympics, upright wrestling persisted
as the competitive form. But what holds were allowed, what
moves and counters were employed, are questions that cannot

be definitely answered. Information on wrestling in antiquity has been culled from scattered literary texts such as quotations of the stoic Epictetus, Pindar's ode to an Isthmian victory, and a dialog by the late Greek satirist Lucian. In addition, portrayals of wrestling on pottery, coins and murals aid the historian. Taken together, however, the information is incomplete, contradictory and definitely open to interpretation.

Information in the following description is generally accepted with minimal controversy. Opponents, oiled and dusted—often with lucky sand brought from home—met in a prepared pit that was covered with sand; "arena" is Latin for sand. Wrestlers were matched by lot, not weight or size. The object was to throw one's opponent three times. Landing on the back, shoulders or perhaps the hips constituted a fall. Grace and style were valued as is suggested by the fact that originally wrestling was accompanied by flute playing. Also Greek dance which was a vigorous and athletic activity widely practiced by young men often included choreographic imitation of the moves of wrestling. There is evidence that holds below the waist were allowed, at least as counter-moves in avoiding a fall, and leghold takedowns were known. Knees could touch the ground without counting as a fall, for the flying mare was a prevalent tactic. Backflips and bridging were prominent and indicate that the struggle often continued on the ground. Around 700 B.C. wrestling is recorded as the final event of the pentathlon. Beginning in the seventeenth Olympiad, wrestling is listed as a separate event in addition to the pentathlon for men; boys' wrestling was added later. Some believe that pentathlon wrestling emphasized more the art of wrestling than the fight or struggle, but no point system was used by the Greeks in deciding a winner. Competition in wrestling was what we would call fair or clean. Pinching, choking and other punishing holds were not allowed; however, the full Nelson seems to have been permitted.

Pankration, the second form of wrestling found in the games, was a no-holds-barred combination of boxing and wrestling fought on an area specially watered down for the agony of the ground struggle. Those who idealize the Greeks are embarrassed by accounts of the violence and popularity of this Greek version of catch-as-catch-can wrestling. Often it is quickly dismissed as a remnant of earlier training for warriors. The fact, however, that the warlike Spartans at times refused to take part in pankration competition at the games would argue against such rationalizing and gives some indication of the brutality involved. Robert Yeager, a modern censor of violence in sports, is blunt in his description: "Borrowing from Egypt and Mesopotamia, they [the Greeks] evolved the Pankration (meaning "all-powerful"), a mixture of boxing and wrestling so savage that it was steadfastly avoided by Milon of Croton, who lived in the sixth century B.C. and was the most famous of all ancient Greek wrestlers. Opponents fought with every part of their bodies and were free to kick, trample and use strangleholds; they could legally dislocate and break the bones of opponents. Though officially banned, eye-gouging frequently is depicted in wall paintings."[6] Pinching, hairpulling, elbowing, and even biting must be added to Yeager's list of crudities that recall the worst sham bouts of professional wrestling today. But in antiquity they were for real as an account of the third Olympic championship won by Arrhacion in 564 B.C. attests. The victor lying atop his opponent who held him in a chokehold so wrenched the other's ankle that the loser signaled defeat. But Arrhachion did not rise to the acclaim of the crowds; he lay motionless, strangled to death.

Originally participation in the games was open to all free Greek males. In the early years regional champions and others vied for the honor of taking part in the harmonious festivals of athletic and artistic competition. The symbolic wreath for the victor was reward enough. But in the seventh century B.C. and clearly by the middle of the fifth century, professionalism entered the games. Hometowns granted victors substantial awards and even tax exemptions and sinecures. Athletes were occasionally recruited to represent a city or district; even talented slaves of questionable Greek origin were at times sent off to represent a town. Amateurs began to lose to full-time professionals. There was a gradual shift from participant to spectator as crowds gathered for the fetes. Important persons strove for the victor's wreath as a crowning career achievement. Their participation, though legitimate, could influence others' decisions to compete as well as their will to win. Philip of Macedon was proud of his victory in the pankration which was legitimately won. But centuries later in the twilight of the ancient Olympics Nero bought off the competition in staging his victories at the games. The historian Gibbon considered the rise of professionalism and the shift to spectator sports one factor in the decline and fall of the Romans, the inheritors of the Greeks.

Wrestling was a part of everyday Greek life and not limited to special occasions such as the games. Youths were educated not only in grammar, rhetoric and mathematics but also in physical training. In the seventh book of laws, Plato prescribed physical education, by which he meant dancing and wrestling for young men: "Anything which comes under 'stand-up wrestling,' exercises in the disengaging of neck, arms and ribs which can be practiced with spirit and gallant bearing to the benefit of strength and health, is serviceable for all occasions and may not be neglected .... All such knowledge shall be generously imparted on the one side [by masters] and gratefully received on the other [by students]."[7] The palaestra was often a privately owned exercise court built onto the house of a schoolmaster for instruction in physical education, especially wrestling. At the palaestra boys were paired up and learned wrestling under the guidance of their instructor. Holds were practiced at first on command, and only after mastering the basics did the youths engage in free matches. Older males sustained the boys' interest and encouraged them to perfect their wrestling skill by scheduling many meets somewhat like little league or scholastic sports today. At the national games, there were events for boys and youths as well as for mature adults. Training and recreation in wrestling was divided into as many as five classes: boys 14 to 16, 16 to 18 and 18 to 20; young men 20 to 30; and finally adults over 30. But there was concern about excessive competition for boys. Aristotle, who noted that few boy champions did well in the games as adults, alerted his countrymen to the evils of too much training and competition in a boy's early years.

Young men beyond school years and older males often met at the public gymnasium or at the palaestra outside of school hours for their own continuing education and for sports.

Several of Plato's dialogs take place in a palaestra which had clubrooms and benches around the exercise courtyard. The gymnasium was a larger public building usually outside of town with areas for track and field events as well as wrestling and boxing arenas. Greek men would invite one another to a workout in wrestling as readily as modern businessmen engage in a friendly game of golf or racketball. Various styles of wrestling were practiced as popular sport throughout antiquity. There were those who limited their play to practicing gymnastic upright wrestling routines as well as those who enjoyed rough and tumble encounters as is evidenced by the Roman Martial sending a friend a leather cap so his hair would not be pulled while wrestling. Plato, whose name "The Broad Shouldered" comes from his grappling days, reportedly once wrestled in the Isthmian Games. The late Roman philosopher emperor Marcus Aurelius delighted, as did Plato, in wrestling in his mature years. But then so did the brutal gladiator emperors Commodus and Caracalla.

Wrestling in antiquity was, of course, not limited to Europe. Reports from early Chinese diplomats, medieval European visitors and more recent colonialists tell of great wrestling tournaments held in Central Asia from time immemorial. The styles still found today in Afghanistan, India, Iran, Mongolia, Pakistan, Turkey and even parts of Yugoslavia all suggest common origins. The contests can be traced back over 600 years to the Turkoman tribes brought by Arabs into their lands as mercenaries who eventually subjugated their masters. Wrestlers, usually wearing leather knee britches and carefully oiled, meet even today in festive tourneys that at times continue for days until a single champion emerges. The matches are conducted in the open or in arenas at time honored locales such as Edirne, the site of the old Roman Adrianople in European Turkey. In 1969, at the 608th "Kirpinar" or national meet at Edirne, there were 727 wrestlers competing. Athletes often belong to clubs where weightwork, ritualized exercises and feats of strength are all integrated into the serious training of future champions. Endurance as well as skill is very important as contests have no time limit or point system and can last for hours. The final championship bout in 1969 had several rest breaks but lasted for 14 hours and 35 minutes of actual wrestling. In the Turkish version, a man loses when his shoulders are pinned; in Iran, a man thrown on his back is vanquished.

In Japan, the preservation by ritual of the ancient wrestling form of sumo gives us unique insight today into a style of sport whose origins are lost in national history and myth. In special schools, young men of exceptional size were trained as apprentices under older masters; this practice continues unbroken today. As a low center of gravity, great girth and prodigious strength are essential to the short, quick-action bouts, the sumatori train and feed on a special rich rice ragout diet so that they reach a bulk of around three hundred pounds. Wrestling is held in two-week tournaments involving fifteen contestants all competing regardless of weight. Competition takes place several times a year in various cities for the Emperor's Cup. Pageantry, ritual and dramatic competition are hallmarks of the round-robin sumo meets. The rules are simple; a man wins if he forces his opponent out of the fifteen-foot sand ring or if any part of his adversary's body other than the feet touches the ground. Referees in Shinto garb signal the start of the quick bursts of belt-type wrestling. Contestants remove elaborate aprons to be clothed only in ropen loincloths which opponents try to grasp for a throw. Before engaging in combat, sumatori perform a simple ritual. After tossing ceremonial sand, they clap their hands to awaken the gods, they raise their arms to show they have no hidden weapons, and they stomp their feet to stamp out evil. Men who win three tournaments or more are usually designated grand champions, of which there can be several at a time. A grand champion receives a white robe in a timeless Shinto rite. It becomes then his honor to perform the opening ceremony at tournaments.

In old India, where wrestling was called the king of manly games, matches continued without rest intervals for hours until one man's shoulders and hips simultaneously touched the ground. Bouts were between opponents selected without regard to age, size or weight. Years of training in endurance, strength, vitality and skill were required of anyone taking the sport seriously. The Great Gama, an Indian champion who toured Europe in 1910, decisively and swiftly defeated the best continental and American wrestlers in public and club bouts. This was no surprise in light of his training regimen of thousands of leg squats, two thousand push-ups, a five-mile run and at least three hours of wrestling every day. Later when nearly fifty years old, he bested the recognized European champion twice in matches that lasted less than a minute. Gama's training schedule is but one document of the fanatical dedication Asian wrestlers gave to their sport which has enjoyed popular and princely support over the centuries.

The Jews of biblical times, though generally uninterested in athletics, were enthusiastic wrestlers. Jacob's bout with a messenger from God is well known. The name of Israel bestowed upon him has been interpreted as "wrestler with God."[8] Even the dietary law prohibiting eating the leg of an animal still containing the sciatic nerve has been traced back to Jacob's dislocated thigh in that bout. The Jews wrestled wearing a distinctive belt which was a prized possession. Leaders were often successful wrestlers as is suggested when Judah is recognized by his staff, signet and belt (Genesis, 38:18). The Messiah is to wear a belt of righteousness (Isaiah, 11:5) that is, to be a wrestling champion in the struggle of good and evil. The frequent biblical injunction to gird one's loins is a metaphor from belt wrestling that attests to the popularity of the sport among the people of ancient Israel.

Early Christians had good reason to shun all athletics since they as outsiders and victims knew only too well the degenerate gladiatorial contests of Rome. Among the early church fathers, Augustine wrote from personal experience when he warned that violent spectator sports could become a debasing, consuming passion. For centuries Christian teaching rejected the flesh, the body, as one of three sources of sin. Christendom had little room for organized sport or bodily exercise. And yet there is much evidence of impromptu popular sport in feudal Europe. Not only did incessant warfare require men skilled in martial exercises, but frequent folk festivals gave natural rise to sporting competition.

Evidence that wrestling was one such sport has been gleaned from unexpected sources. Illuminated capitals in manuscripts depict grapplers. Figures of wrestlers carved into choir stalls and chiseled into the stonework of medieval churches are lasting records of a popular activity. A document from England in 1258 reads: "We also decree that the clergy proclaim in their churches that no one is to take it on himself to engage in wrestling, ring-dancing or in any other kinds of dishonest gaming, especially on church feast-days."[9] The word "especially" suggests the censored activities that could not be rooted out but at least might be restricted to profane times and places. Thirty years later another text repeats the injunction: "We strictly enjoin parish priests to announce publicly in their churches that no one presume to practice wrestling, ring-dancing or any other dishonest games in cemeteries, especially on vigils and feast days." These prohibitions are clear evidence that wrestling was a popular activity engaged in by commoners when they gathered together on holidays. Village wakes and fairs were other occasions in medieval life for sports such as wrestling, races, archery and proto-football matches.

How profoundly and lastingly wrestling permeated folk culture and literature both then and later on a mythological basis can be seen in the fifteenth century in Mallory's *Morte D'Arthur*. In this poem Gawain represents the old and Lancelot the new order. In the titanic struggle between these two heroes Gawain's strength waxes in the morning, Lancelot's in the afternoon, but the great conflict between the two comes in a titanic wrestling match when Lancelot realizes that Gawain's strength comes from the contact of his feet with the earth and he therefore lifts Gawain's feet from mother— and strength-giving—earth and holds him up while his strength fades. The power of this symbolism is evidenced in much literature, including Herman Melville's 1853 short story "Bartleby" and continued in his thinking throughout his life as long as he thought of supermen/women and heroes. For example, in his last story, "Billy Budd," Melville talks about the Handsome Sailor as being no dandy but "a mighty boxer or wrestler" with both "strength and beauty."

Documents from Italy in the third century A.D. record an early revival of the Olympics. These were folk meets open to all comers with contests in running and wrestling; later, horse races replaced foot events. But it is in medieval France and England where the sources of modern wrestling are to be found. The Bretons were especially noted for their strength and skill in a form of upright wrestling that allowed no grips below the waist, and no legholds or tripping. This is the origin of what eventually emerged as Greco-Roman wrestling. The farmers of Brittany regularly practiced wrestling and jousting on Sunday afternoons. Because matches took place in public with women among the interested spectators, medieval wrestlers were fully clothed. The Bretons believed in fair sport. They met after making the sign of the cross, shook hands, promised to be friends whatever the outcome, and assured each other that they carried no magic charms and had not signed a pact with the devil to win.[10] By the Hundred Years' War the English were well acquainted with the prowess of French wrestlers. It is recorded that during a truce in 1402, international games were held between the warring parties in jousting, battle-ax contests and wrestling. There is evidence that matches between members of different classes were allowed in wrestling, for noblemen were quite proud of victories over powerful yeomen.

In Britain, wrestling skill has been traced back to the arm-lock Beowulf used to conquer Grendel.[11] By the Middle Ages, the Englishmen in the various counties had developed different types of wrestling. The men of Lancashire preferred a loose or freestyle which is most similar to modern American amateur style in the initial stance taken, the great variety of holds and escapes employed, the pinning of both shoulders to determine victory. Kicking, grabbing of clothing or hair, pinching or punishing holds were prohibited. There is one variant of loose wrestling that was mainly an upright contest, for a man lost if any part of his body other than the feet, knees or hands touched the ground. In Devonshire and Cornwall, booted contestants started the bout with kicking, tripping and savate-like blows before locking up in close combat. Holds as in judo consisted in grasping the sleeve and the back of an opponent's jacket and then trying to toss him to the ground in a three-point landing; that is, both shoulders and one hip or one shoulder and both hips. In Cumberland and Westmoreland, backhold wrestling dating to the days of the Vikings was in vogue. Contestants took a stance with one arm over and one arm under the other man's shoulders. Hands remained locked behind the adversary's back as both struggled to toss or force the other to the ground. If a man lost his grip or if any part of his body other than the feet touched the ground, he lost the fall. If both fell to the ground at the same time, the fall was a "dogfall" and had to be repeated. In modern times such bouts often run a half hour with many falls, most of them dogfalls, until three clean falls can be scored by one contestant.

Besides local contests on special occasions, annual wrestling competitions were held in London by the time of the Plantagenets. They were scheduled for certain feast days such as St. James, St. Bartholomew and, surprisingly, even Good Friday. Sponsors and contestants would decide on the style of wrestling to be used. Winners and other skillful participants received prizes, often a gamecock or a plumed hat or even a ram as Chaucer says of his miller: "At wrastlynge he wolde have alwey the Ram."[12] As in other countries, an outstanding wrestler might catch the eye of his sovereign and join the royal retinue as a professional wrestler for courtly entertainment and international meets. The most famous such meet attended negotiations between Henry VIII and Francis I at a festival on the Field of the Cloth of Gold in 1520. As part of the entertainment, seven wrestlers from each nation were matched up. The English won handily over the French who had failed to bring along their Breton champions. Accounts vary as to what followed. According to one version, at the end of the matches as Henry gloated, Francis became so enraged that he jumped up and took hold of the English king. Attendants quickly separated the two monarchs. In another version, it is said that Henry challenged Francis who was five years his senior: "Brother, we wolle wrestle." To save face the French king accepted. Henry gained quick advantage with his superior strength and athletic ability. But then, using his long legs to maneuver, Francis worked himself free and grabbing Henry's game leg pinned him. No second fall is recorded as the banquet table was set and waiting.

In the waning Middle Ages and dawning Renaissance, wrestling remained a sport popular particularly in the countryside among the rural folk as a document issued by Queen Elizabeth in 1569 verifies. John Powlter received a license to organize Sunday games in Middlesex including "...the Lepping for Men, the Running for Men, the Wrastlinge, the Throwing of the Sledge and the Pytchinge of the Barre,

with all such other games as have at any time heretofore or now
be licensed, used or played."[13] Londoners still took interest in
the holiday tournaments as an entry in the famous *Pepy's
Diary* suggests: "Went to Moorefields ... and saw the
wrestling ... between the north and west countrymen."[14]
Wrestling persisted well into the eighteenth century, along
with cudgel playing and rough football matches, as standard
activity at country wakes and fairs. But in the cities and larger
towns wrestling gradually fell from favor and was relegated to
beer gardens and low taverns. Still Milton in his 1644 study on
education recommended wrestling: "They [youths] must be
also practiz'd in all locks and gripes of wrestling."
Nevertheless, elaborate rules of etiquette discouraged the
upper class from engaging themselves in crude sports and
particularly from competing with rowdy commoners.

Among the gentry wrestling did persist but only as
training tertiary in importance to skill in fencing and
horsemanship. Two records, however, survive as interesting
evidence of the skill needed and the holds employed when
gentlemen did wrestle. The documents could be seen as
bookends to the historical age of courtly manners. First there is
a series of sketches by Albrecht Durer which the Emperor
Maximilian commissioned. They were to be etched onto plates
for a printed manual on fencing and wrestling. Durer drew 120
wrestling maneuvers and jotted down verbal glosses, but the
manual was never published. Two centuries later toward the
end of the courtly era,a country squire, Sir Thomas Parkyns,
published a book called *The Inn-Play or Cornish-Hugg
Wrestler*. In a rambling text, Parkyns advocated the
strengthening and training of youths by wrestling masters as
was done in fencing. "Legs and Hands are not made for Cards
and Dancing only," he scoffs at young fops unfit for the service
of their country. He himself had learned in public school at
Westminster and later at Cambridge the superiority of "in-
style" wrestling which he called "Cornish," not as a
geographic designation but in honor of an instructor by that
name who knew 500 holds and counters. Parkyns rejected the
kicking and boxing blows of "out-wrestling" and pointed to the
superior skill and exercise found in locking up with an
opponent in a style reminiscent of ancient Greek upright

wrestling. Parkyns suggested regular instruction in the sport for young men. To this end he conducted annual tournaments at his own expense for many years. Participants, matched by lot, grappled until one gained three falls and was declared the winner. Matches continued until a tournament champion could be determined and awarded a handsome hat worth 22 shillings. Parkyns, who knew only too well the dissolute ways of some of the young gentlemen, strictly warned gamesters against bribing a poorer but better opponent into throwing a match.

On this continent many tribes of native Americans practiced wrestling long before the first European settlers came. Unlike the balancing exercise called Indian wrestling in the old Boy Scout handbooks, the serious contest was a rough encounter. At the start of a match opponents gripped each other above the hips. All moves and holds including kicking and arm twisting were allowed as contestants struggled to bring each other to the ground. As soon as a part of the body other than the feet touched the ground, an athlete lost. It has been said that skilled Indian wrestlers would travel about from tribe to tribe making a profession of their art.

The spotty record of pastimes in colonial America includes occasional mention of wrestling. In New England, farm folk celebrated any time they gathered for business, work or play such as election days, barn raisings, harvesting, fairs and huskings. Besides heightening their pleasure at being together in song, dance and rum, Americans were competing at marksmanship, foot races and wrestling as early as 1680.[15] In the South the aristocratic distinctions from Old England influenced both the choice of sport—horse racing was the most popular—and who might play. Ordinary people did divert themselves occasionally as participants but often both slave and commoner were relegated to the role of spectator at horse races and cockfights held at fairs and on plantations. Sir Francis Nicolson, while posting prizes in 1691 for marksmanship, swordsmanship, horse and foot races and wrestling, stipulated "all which prizes are to be shott for and played for by the better sort of Virginians only, who are Batchelors."[16]

American folklore from the early days of the Republic up to

the Civil War knows tales of the wrestling prowess of its men. Rough and tumble bouts and even pankration encounters came naturally to a people pushing back the frontier and tilling the soil. George Washington, while studying at the academy in Fredericksburg, gained repute as a wrestler skilled in the gentlemanly "common British" style. It has been recorded that at age forty-six, "the Commander of the Continental Armies summoned enough of his old form to deal flying mares to seven saucy volunteers from Massachusetts."[17] Young Abe Lincoln, as every school child once knew, was a local champion in the free-for-all wrestling favored on the frontier. Lincoln typified early rural American wrestling in which an out of town challenger took on a local strongman. After sufficient wagers were placed, the local hero usually would lose a close match rather than be overwhelmed by the itinerant grappler. Lincoln worked the Ohio and Mississippi river areas and engaged in about three hundred matches from 1828 on until politics denied him the time to continue wrestling. Records of American westward expansion are replete with descriptions of one-eyed brawlers, earless innkeepers, and others who bore scars from pankration bouts. Mark Twain in *Life on the Mississippi* tells the yarn of a self-proclaimed champion from Arkansas nicknamed "Sudden Death and General Desolation" who challenged all comers and struck fear in many by his boasting alone.

It was not on the American frontier, however, but in a quiet farming area of Vermont where skillful wrestling, collar and elbow or scuffling, was perfected. Eventually it was this style that would most influence the development of modern American wrestling, both amateur and professional. From the 1830s on, Irish immigrants began to settle in good numbers in the northwest corner of Vermont. They brought their traditional wrestling that had much in common with that advocated by Sir Thomas Parkyns as "in-wrestling" and those styles called Cornish, square-hold or box wrestling. Back on the Old Sod the Irish, whom penal laws had long forbidden to wear weapons, developed self-defense skills. It was not uncommon for a town or village to maintain a champion scuffler as an informal community constable. Bullies at times held towns in their grip until a new champion dethroned them in fights that could end in death. By the time the Irish came to Vermont, their scuffling had been refined to a recreational pastime that still occasionally was used to settle quarrels. The first priests sent to minister to the new settlers were Irishmen themselves who had all, by chance, "fingered the collar" before taking orders. They advocated the sport for youthful recreation and also as a controlled means of resolving the disputes that developed among members of their flock. County conflicts from the old homeland as well as new rivalries and feuds gave plenty of opportunity for serious scuffling. But most often it was a simple source of recreation for the immigrant farmers and blacksmiths when they gathered for mass, at fairs or outside country taverns. Irish scuffling was quickly learned by other Green Mountain Men since it emphasized skill over brutality and injuries were rare.

The name collar and elbow came from the initial boxlike stance taken by the wrestlers. To prevent kicking, rushes and stalling, opponents started by facing each other with one hand on the other's shoulder and one on his elbow. Though similar to the modern referee's hold, the initial lockup differed in that the wrestlers held their heads upright as they tried to unbalance or toss the other while they circled clockwise. Leglifts and shooting were possible after the initial stance, but a wrestler was not to loosen the starting hold voluntarily. Ground wrestling followed with bridging and evasive moves until one man was pinned at all four points, that is, both shoulders and hips touched the ground at the same time. As in most earlier forms of wrestling, feeling out an opponent could last for quite some time until one man was thrown or lost his balance, and so matches often lasted an hour or longer with no breaks or rest periods. As timing, balance, endurance, footwork and quickness were the marks of a good scuffler, a small adept man could win over a larger or stronger but unskilled opponent. This was true sport, for skill and practice determined the outcome rather than brute strength or foul play.

Collar and elbow scuffling would have been lost to history had it not been for the Civil War. In that poor man's war, officers would select athletic youths and give them orders to train squads in wrestling which was the sport chosen since no equipment was needed. Stripped to the waist and shoeless, they set to and both learned and taught each other the natural way. Those regiments with men already trained such as the Vermonters gained repute among the troops and passed their art on to others who saw that a skilled little wrestler could win over an inept larger man. It is no surprise that a Vermont native, George William Flagg, became the wrestling champion of the Army of the Potomac. Charles Wilson in his study quickly sketches the growth of wrestling after the war: "It spread through the Union Army during the Civil War as casual recreation for fun or glory and in the 1880s was drawing thousands of dollars in side bets and big money gates from Boston and New York, through Detroit and out to San Francisco. By 1888 scufflers from Ireland were coming to Vermont to learn collar and elbow and thereby graduating to championships back home ... even while wrestlers from the Green Mountains were working their respective ways to London, Buenos Aires and Sydney for the purpose of latching on to further international laurels."[18] The growth of wrestling from rural American pastime to international event is but one reflection of the many changes that were taking place in the United States during the late nineteenth century.

With the growth of cities and the spread of information via newspapers and magazines, a public for spectator events including sports had already developed in antebellum America. Sporting journals and newspaper accounts sparked interest in all types of races—turf, pedestrian, rowing and even yachting—prior to the Civil War. It cannot be glossed over that betting played a significant role in raising interest among the general populace and the participants. The bareknuckle prize ring also attracted attention as papers reported the results of significant fights both in America and in England. *Harper's Weekly* and other respected journals devoted coverage to the tours of English fighters and to east coast contests. In 1853 the *New York Clipper,* modeled on a British journal, became the first American bible for the prize ring. The New York press reported crowds numbering as many as 6000 at some early fights. But wrestling as a rural sport was ignored; only occasional mention of a local kicking contest or other rough brawl made it to print.

An ambivalent attitude toward sport evolved in the young

American republic that still lingers today. Especially in New England there was concern that in developing a sound mind in a sound body, as muscular Christianity advocated, youth not fall prey to the vices of the flesh—not to mention drinking, cussing and gambling. Ever since the publication of *Tom Brown's School Days,* group activities such as rowing and pedestrianism were seen as positive participant sports that could properly channel the vitality of future leaders. Academies and colleges both in England and America incorporated sportclubs within their walls for their select students. The YMCA soon extended its original missionary activity by offering the benefits of wholesome exercise and participatory sport to less monied middle-class youths. Participation is a key to understanding the end desired; conformity within group activity would restrain rugged individualism and would mold proper gentlemen. The ideal was amateurism. In contrast, individualistic activities such as prize fighting and wrestling were at the time early spectator sports that led to professionalism and attracted the gambling set, the unruly crowd. While the papers reported bareknuckle fights, they also condemned them. As late as 1890, prize fighting was illegal in more than a dozen states. Horse racing, that other unruly spectator sport, was a passion so popular with individuals from all classes that the muscular Christians and proper Victorians had to content themselves with banning Sunday events.

The beginnings of professional wrestling, and incidentally of baseball, as a sport can be traced back to the returning Civil War veterans. Many of them had learned these recreations while in the army and had cheered on their champions and teams in regimental contests. While some had learned Vermont scuffling or participated in freestyle wrestling bouts, most serious contests in the service had been the classic strongman versus strongman bulling bouts soon to be known as Greco-Roman wrestling. This was essentially the same style as that perfected by the old Bretons which made its way eventually into the modern Olympics.

Postbellum America was the first real sporting era in our history. In a nation developing a love for sports, wrestling bouts between local champions brought out the crowds.

Wrestling helped fill a void, for most modern spectator sports were not yet devised in a day when walking contests were the rage of the country. To be sure, there was fledgling professional baseball in the 1870s, but no football as yet or basketball. In the growing cities commercialized sports including prize fighting, wrestling, pedestrianism and bicycle riding attracted paying customers. Interest was heightened by growing newspaper coverage of local events as well as by telegraphed reports from around the country and by cabled sporting news from England. *The National Police Gazette,* which in the 1880s became the most widely distributed sports weekly in America, gave full coverage to wrestling, boxing and other spectator sports. James Gordon Bennett, Jr. devoted full columns of his *New York Herald* to sports by the late 1860s. Personally he was a follower and advocate of wrestling in its beginnings in New York City. He played an important role in the growth of professional wrestling, for there are several prerequisites for a modern professional sport. Not least among these is media coverage. Interested spectators who are willing to pay becomes as essential as the athletes themselves, and it is the coverage given by the media that creates fans. Professional sport also needs middlemen, those who provide a place for the event, regulate the sport, arrange contests, advertise and take financial risks. In postbellum New York all the requisites for wrestling to evolve as a professional sport came together.

The central figure in the story is William Muldoon, known as "The Solid Man of Sport." As a powerfully built young soldier, he had been selected to wrestle as his unit's representative in various army meets during the Civil War. After the service, rather than return to the farm, he went through a series of heavy labor jobs in New York City. Early along in his city days, he learned a promising athletically built man could pick up extra money by fighting in bareknuckle bouts staged in the rough taverns of the Bowery district. The victorious pugilist would receive three dollars; the loser, two. After winning one bareknuckle fight, Muldoon switched to wrestling because the purses were greater given the longer contest; seven dollars to the winner, three to the loser. It was in wrestling matches at the most famous and infamous Houston

Street establishment, Harry Hill's, that Muldoon began his career. Starting in the 1860s, on payday Hill's customers would chip in a quarter each to set up a purse for a backroom wrestling match or fistfight. Soon Hill and other owners saw the profit in building stagehalls onto their taverns and putting up their own purses for the bouts. The sporting bar became very popular with men of all classes. Harry Hill counted Thomas Edison, P.T. Barnum and editors such as Fox of the *Police Gazette* and Bennett of the *Herald* among his patrons and friends. Edison later installed the first electric hall lighting system in Hill's establishment for fights, vaudeville farces, circus acts and strongman feats.

So it was at Hill's nefarious saloon that the requisites for professional sport, in this case for wrestling, came together. There were men of the press to give coverage to matches, to stir up interest, to proclaim champions. There was Harry himself who provided the arena and carried the costs. But even more importantly, Harry set house rules and on occasion refereed so that the contest would be fair lest the rugged betting fans become an unruly mob. And of course there was a popular young star, Bill Muldoon.

Throughout his long and colorful life, Muldoon remained at heart a health buff and physical culturist. He had learned upright wrestling by happenstance during the war and practiced his skill as an opportunist at Harry Hill's emporium. In 1870 he headed off to volunteer on the French side in the Franco-Prussian War but arrived too late. During a short stay in Paris he attended Greco-Roman bouts and observed strongman acts to perfect his knowledge before returning to New York and his friends at Harry's. The publisher Bennett, who also had toured Europe and become fascinated by the Greco-Roman matches he witnessed there, convinced Muldoon that he should concentrate on the continental style and proclaim himself the contending American champion. Muldoon liked the idea; for his part, Bennett aided his protege by arranging regular employment for him as a member of New York's finest. Meanwhile Bennett went to Vermont to encourage several other good wrestlers, among them the old champion of the Army of the Potomac, George Flagg, to use the press to issue and accept wrestling challenges.

Back in New York, Muldoon won recognition by handily defeating the reigning police force champion in wrestling. This feat led to a bout in January 1880 at Gilmore's Gardens, the first Madison Square Gardens, in which Muldoon met Thiebaud Bauer to determine the Greco-Roman championship. Muldoon won the gold medal donated by a sports journal in a bout that drew over 3000—a sizable crowd in those days. That there was great interest in the match is evident by the fact that the *Times* devoted six paragraphs in its coverage, an unheard of amount of print for a sport event at that time. Harry Hill served as referee in the two out of three fall match. The wrestlers struggled for forty-three minutes before Muldoon gained the first fall; in the second, Bauer maneuvered his opponent's shoulders into momentary contact with the mat after twenty minutes; finally, Muldoon dropped and pinned his adversary after only three minutes for the deciding fall.

Here is not the place to recount in detail Muldoon's years as champion. But some further episodes point out problems that have remained with professional wrestling ever since its birth in the Bowery. Muldoon's first title defense against William Miller, a fellow stage strongman, pugilist and wrestler, was a dull though evenly fought match that dragged on more than six hours and ended in a draw. Fair epic struggles, unfortunately, do not bring back paying customers. The question was and is, how can the action be enlivened and lead to a decisive timely outcome without rigging the match. Muldoon's three clashes with Clarence Whistler, a former iron worker from Omaha, showed there was national interest in wrestling, but these too were lengthy struggles indicative more of the wrestlers' endurance and ability to shed blood while suffering agonizingly painful holds than contests of skill. Other questions arose: what limits should be placed on standoff situations where neither man can work to a pin. What role, if any, should punishing or submission holds have in the sport? Also, though bloodshed has attracted a certain clientele ever since the days of the Greeks, should it be permitted, or faked or even encouraged in the sport? As Muldoon's fame spread, he was challenged by other champions from near and far. Edwin Bibby, a middleweight from England skilled at catch as catch can, met him for the Greco-Roman title.

Muldoon, a strongman of over 200 pounds, easily defeated his smaller opponent. Is it fair to match up men of different weight and size? In many early bouts arguments arose among seconds as to whether or not a fall had been scored. What rules or style of wrestling shall be employed?

In 1881 Muldoon resigned from the police force to tour the country in wrestling bouts and exhibitions. For many years on regular tours with other wrestlers including Miller, Whistler and Bibby in tow, Muldoon remained undefeated in visits to Pittsburgh, Cincinnati, St. Louis, Chicago, New Orleans, Denver, San Francisco and other growing cities. The troupe performed in varied settings from music hall and vaudeville stage to carnival tent. They put on exhibition bouts, strongman demonstrations and matches with local challengers in freestyle and Greco-Roman wrestling. All the hoopla of modern professional wrestling as a roadshow attraction was there. The media build-up before bouts and challenges issued in the local press, claimants to regional titles, a collection of impressive championship belts, foreign challengers, colorful tights and even costumes were all part of the wrestling scene in the 1880s. Yet wrestling in that day enjoyed a fairly good reputation despite the carnival atmosphere, especially when compared to fisticuffs. A New Orleans journalist suggested it could become a popular sport with young gymnasts. After a visit to that city in 1883 by Muldoon and his company of American and foreign athletes, the *Picayune* reporter endorsed the sport: "A wrestling match is one of the most commendable of athletic exhibitions as there is but little brutality connected with it, and agility, coolness, strength and science are the winning points."[19] It must be remembered that wrestling was in the carnival tent and on the music hall stage because those were the public arenas of the day for spectator events. Gymnasiums, sporthalls, municipal arenas, auditoriums and superdomes dedicated exclusively to sport had not as yet been dreamed up.

Through all the contests, exhibitions and genuine bouts, Muldoon remained undefeated and, more importantly, remained generally recognized as Greco-Roman champion. In 1887 at age 48 he announced his retirement as champion after an exhibition at Miner's Theatre in the Bowery and proclaimed

Ernest Roeber, a younger man in his troupe, the new world champion. That did not mean Muldoon was done with wrestling, for he occasionally entered the ring in exhibitions and trained for several serious bouts such as his defeat of Ivan Lewis, the original "Strangler" Lewis, at Christmas time in Philadelphia in 1889. In fairness to Lewis, it should be mentioned that this was a Greco-Roman match, and Lewis was a champion in freestyle. After passing on the championship, Muldoon diversified his interests. He trained John L. Sullivan, whom he had defeated in a boxer versus wrestler match in 1887. Later Muldoon toured with theater groups including the Barrymores as Charles, the wrestler in *As You Like It*. Finally, he established a health institute, a reducing farm, for captains of industry, celebrities and other wealthy patrons before capping his career as the first New York Commissioner of Boxing. Muldoon, one of the first professional American athletes, emerged from the game of wrestling financially secure and respected.

Wrestling in postbellum America was not limited to the Greco-Roman championship held in New York City. The frontier continued to produce rugged freestyle brawls in which wrestlers fought for side bets and an occasional championship belt. The men from Vermont, too, in ever greater numbers practiced collar and elbow scuffling and developed championships in loose weight classes at annual tournaments for amateurs. At a GAR gathering in Great Bethel in 1876, over 1200 men scuffled for medals and prizes; at the Roxbury Volunteers Wrestling Tournament of 1885, 300 entrants came to wrestle for fun and to make wagers on the side. Many of the Vermont wrestlers ventured out of state, especially to the midwest and the far west to ply their sport and to garner winnings. A champion Vermonter, Henry Dufor, settled down in the haberdashery business in Massachusetts, but he regularly posted $100 challenges in newspapers for worthy scuffling opponents. John McMahon made several trips from Vermont to California where he became Pacific Coast Champion.

Big James McLaughlin of Detroit had been his regimental champion during the war and had won enough crippling freestyle bouts and significant wagers to declare himself the

Champion of the West. At the Boston Music Hall on a December eve in 1876, he quickly learned the superiority of collar and elbow style when he lost to Jim Owens, a Vermont beltholder who was 75 pounds lighter and five inches shorter. This bout, which was fought for $1000 and the collar and elbow championship of the world, signaled the beginning of the spread of collar and elbow techniques into American freestyle wrestling. *The Police Gazette* sponsored matches in the style and even awarded Jim Owens a championship belt in collar and elbow. The belt did not long remain uncontested. It is significant for the spread of scuffling that Muldoon hired on collar and elbow men for his travelling troupes.

P.T. Barnum, who had learned a bit about wrestling at Harry Hill's saloon, signed up a scuffler, Ed Decker, who later won the *Police Gazette* belt in collar and elbow style in 1887. Barnum found Decker ideal for his purposes, for at five foot six and just over 150 pounds he looked deceptively vulnerable. "The circus posted an open offer of $100 to anyone who could 'throw' the Little Wonder from Vermont, and $50 to anybody who could remain upright in the ring with him for three minutes. The circus never had to pay a cent," Wilson reports.[20] Decker soon ran out of challengers so Barnum added John McMahon to his entourage. McMahon, a Vermonter, had wrestled in the west after the war. He even left his farm in 1884 to work his way to England to beat a self-styled world's champion in just over five minutes. In Barnum's circus Decker and McMahon were gaudily outfitted to wrestle daily in twenty-minute prearranged bouts. One day Ed was the champion, the next Jim appeared with the emblem of eminence and pinned his adversary. In two years of touring and 300 encounters, the two never really did find out who was the better scuffler. The bouts won by various Vermont wrestlers around their country, their travels in circus and roadshow, their proof that skill is superior to brute strength—all influenced the evolution of American freestyle wrestling.

There is a dictum that those who give birth to a sport and control its development determine what it is to become. This may be accurate when applied to modern professional entertainment sports from yachting, golf and tennis to roller derby. It is doubtful, however, that the founding fathers of wrestling in the gaslit era ever intended it to be professional sport in any modern sense. For that matter, could the luminaries of academe in the nineteenth century ever have foreseen the monster intercollegiate athletics would one day become? To be sure, there is much to lament in the way professional wrestling developed from the 1880s until around 1910, and much of what happened then still influences the game today. But maybe it would be more insightful to see what wrestling was rather than measure the modern professional entertainment against theoretical norms for sport.

Wrestling, like boxing, grew on the fringe of respectable society. Both were and are fairly natural contests as their long histories attest; proving who is the best man around is a basic contest. When drinking and betting crowds gather, such contests naturally arise. Harry Hill, Owney Goeghagan and the other tavern owners of New York may have had a shrewd eye for a profit when they first set up rings for bouts, but they also established rudimentary rules for the sport. Their promotions, whatever their motives, encouraged the practice and refinement of wrestling whether Greco-Roman, collar and elbow, or catch as catch can. Referees were at hand to agree on style, rules, rest periods and other particulars with the contestants and their seconds or corner judges as they were then called. As in boxing, the referees and seconds a wrestler chose were often selected because they were respected men in the community such as judges, publishers and celebrities. It was necessary to create order for the contest in an era that antidated rulebooks, national regulatory sporting associations and all the organizational paraphernalia that soon was to smother the spontaneity of sport, both amateur and professional.

Team sports, whether club, school or professional, almost immediately need organization—leagues, schedules, regulatory bodies—or they disintegrate into bickering and chaos. They depend upon supporters, spectators who identify with the club or attend the school or live in the city the team purports to represent. But wrestling evolved like boxing as an individual sport with little local identification and no immediate need for regulatory boards to set schedules, arrange meets and debate rules. In the early days of both sports, such matters were determined for each encounter by the athletes themselves and their backers. The very independence of the sport left it open to all the controversy, conflicting championships and suspect contests still found in boxing today. Also in both professional wrestling and boxing there was no natural season, no right occasion. They were and are hit-and-miss sports which depend upon monied promoters and travelling athletes to arrange contests. Wrestlers and boxers lacked the stability of a homecourt since there were not enough athletes in any one locale for continued competition, for a league or a tournament. Wrestlers thus joined vaudeville and travelling shows, the circus and fair circuits of America in the 1880s and '90s when even actors, musicians and opera stars regularly toured the nation to survive at their trade. Wrestlers staged exhibition bouts, performed strongman feats and engaged in genuine matches on Main Street, USA in company with other entertainers in that day long before radio and television when all Americans came "to see the elephant." The relationship between promoters or booking agents and the early wrestling fraternity grew quite naturally. Of course the alliance easily led to bogus bouts, fleecing the betting public and an ever increasing emphasis on show over sport.

To appreciate the problems faced by professional wrestling in the early days, a glance at the flourishing sport scene of the 1970s is helpful. Several examples illustrate how difficult it is for individual sports, unlike team sports, to survive in the entertainment marketplace. Shortlived indeed were the professional track and field roadshow and the professional tennis league. Even some former collegiate and Olympian wrestling greats announced in 1975 that legitimate professional wrestling would soon tour a circuit of cities where the amateur sport drew crowds such as Ann Arbor, Philadelphia, Chicago, Iowa City, Oklahoma City and Cleveland. The promotion was stillborn. Sporting purists and idealists were disappointed in each instance and rationalized the failures away in post-mortem analyses of managerial bungling, athletes' greed, market saturation, public indifference or whatever. Unlike the TV matmen of today and the promoters of the past, all failed to develop their own public and then in good show business tradition give that public what they want the spectators to want.

It must also be remembered that both boxing and wrestling as professional athletic entertainments had quite a different history than most other sports. They were, for one thing, older than most other sports and, more importantly, individual rather than team activities. In the era of Victorian propriety especially, "too many Americans associated the ring and the mat with gamblers, parasites, riff-raff, and the pugs."[21] Both sports represented forces in society that the upper classes in England and America wished to tame and domesticate. Burly sports did not fit into the selectivity of the gentleman's athletic club, early YMCA exercise programs or fledgling collegiate sports. There was a pagan delight in display of muscle, in the strongman stunts, the braggadocio, and even scanty costumes of wrestlers that offended the nice people, those who advocated muscular Christianity in the schools and promoted Victorian team sports in public. Also wrestling and boxing as immediately intelligible contests quickly attracted the immigrant hordes as participants and spectators. The new arrivals were changing both the ethnic mix and the labor force in America. For all these reasons the ruling set saw wrestling and boxing as manifestations of forces in America they disliked, feared and could no longer control. Blue laws against boxing, in particular, helped make it the domain of the outlaw element; wrestling, for its part, developed in the domain of theatrical showmen such as Muldoon, P.T. Barnum and the English impressario C.B. Cochran.[22]

Professional wrestling in America was even in its early days influenced by developments in other countries. Though the concept of modern sport evolved principally in the Anglo-Saxon world, still events on the continent contributed to the emergence of certain sports and to the modern Olympic Movement, of course. Philosophically, sport is a grandchild of the Renaissance with its interest in antiquity; socially, it is the child of two revolutions, the French and the industrial. In the one, the individual began to develop as a person equal to others and freer to pursue his own interests. In the industrial revolution, the shift from countryside to city and the breakdown of old associations such as guilds created a need for new forms of companionship and of socializing. As examples, there were the Turners in Germany, the Sokol physical exercise movement in Bohemia, and the student dueling fraternities—all of which were born in the Napoleonic era.[23] Philosophers, poets and educators including Rousseau, Pestalozzi, Goethe, Byron and Kant theorized that the mind is improved if the body is exercised. Fichte advocated sports teachers trained in anatomy to promote bodily exercises and wrestling. Decades later, the pessimistic philosopher Schopenhauer advised exercise for those whose work was sedentary; he prescribed spending two hours a day at such vigorous activities as brisk walking, cold swims, hiking, wrestling, jumping, dancing, fencing and riding.

By the 1880s American wrestlers, as the first professional athletes, were travelling to demonstrate their prowess and to meet foreign competition in Argentina, Australia and especially Europe. It has been mentioned that Muldoon learned much about Greco-Roman wrestling during his stay in Paris in 1870. In France the old Norman, Breton or Greco-Roman style had survived over the centuries as a sporting activity and as an occasional spectator event as an amusing anecdote from the 1830s shows. An English gentleman of means while in Paris accepted a challenge to wrestle a French baron: "Mr. Jorrocks ungirded his sword and depositing with his frock coat in the cab .... Mr. Jorrocks' action was not very capital, his jackboots and leathers rather impeding his limbs, while the Baron had as little on him as decency would allow."[24] Evidently the French nobleman was more experienced in stylish wrestling at a time when wrestling in England primarily remained a country bumpkin's sport. As late as the 1890s just prior to the canonization of Greco-Roman style in the modern Olympics, an English author could sneer: "Among the different styles of wrestling, the French system for downright absurdity bears off the palm."[25]

Absurd or not, during the belle epoque in Europe, Greco-Roman wrestling matches and exhibitions had evolved into such a popular entertainment that regular tournaments came into vogue. Strongmen performers from athletic clubs, stage shows and circuses gathered from around the world at the annual contests held in Paris, Vienna, Berlin and other major cities. Art nouveau posters on kiosks announced the tournament; postcard sketches and photographs of the stars and the action made early wrestlers the first trading-card athletes. Most of these men were physical culturists and weightlifters as well as wrestlers. They modeled for photographers and for artists and sculptors such as Rodin in poses reminiscent of classical statuary. Their matches and tournaments, too, evoked the ancient Greek games and thus were reputable entertainment. International professional wrestling came into its own in that era of the first world fairs and international competition with gold medals for everything from architecture to beer. Glittering belts and medals for outstanding wrestlers were just part of the showy scene.

Foremost among the respected continental wrestlers was George Hackenschmidt who was born in Russia in 1878. While exercising one day at an athletic club, the naturally gifted young man caught the attention of a physical culturist, Dr. von Krajewski. The doctor took the 19 year old Hackenschmidt to St. Petersburg to supervise his development in gymnastics and weight training. By age 20 Hackenschmidt stood five foot nine and displayed 215 pounds of classically chiseled muscle. Though little experienced in wrestling, in 1898 he defeated a Frenchman, Paul Pons, who was traveling in Russia as the recognized amateur heavyweight Greco-Roman champion. That bout launched Hackenschidt's career as a wrestler. In June 1900 he won the Czar's Tournament which was a prestigious contest in which all serious entrants received 500 French francs in gold. Hackenschmidt, who entered late, quickly defeated the Belgian contender in five minutes, a Bulgarian giant in ten, a French entrant in seven, the Mighty Cossack in ten, a Spaniard in 29 seconds, and the reigning German titleholder in 26 minutes to become the champion. By September he had won the finalist's purse in amazingly quick bouts at two other international meets in Dresden and Budapest. Hackenschmidt's credentials were established. In 1901, after triumphing in meets in the imperial capitals of Berlin and Vienna, he went on to the prestigious tournament in Paris which attracted 130 wrestlers from 31 countries. In elimination matches Hackenschmidt defeated 13 opponents and was proclaimed the world's heavyweight champion in

Greco-Roman style.

Though Hackenschmidt, "The Russian Lion," had become the most famous wrestler and strongman performer on the continent, he was still unknown in the British Isles. So accompanied by other wrestlers he went to England where exhibitions and championship bouts were drawing well in the heady days of the British Empire. It was at the Alhambra Theatre in London that Hackenschmidt first drew public attention. An American, Jack Carkeek, whom Hackenschmidt knew from the continent as a capable wrestler, was challenging all comers as part of a stage revue. Hackenschmidt issued a challenge that was ignored until one night he and his party showed up at the Alhambra and offered Carkeek 25 pounds sterling if the continental champion could not throw the American three times in 15 minutes. Carkeek and his backers knew better than to accept and had the police eject the Russian and his party, but Hackenschmidt gained the attention he wanted. He quickly learned freestyle wrestling and toured the British halls himself. He became very popular. Charles B. Cochran, the famous agent of such theater stars as Sarah Bernhardt, Eleanora Duse and Houdini, booked him in 1902 to play the lead in a light farce, *Sporting Sampson,* that soon folded. But Cochran quickly recouped his losses by arranging the first bout between Hackenschmidt and the original "Terrible Turk," Madrali. A series of matches between the two created much excitement and filled the Olympia and Albert Halls. In 1905 Hackenschmidt even travelled to America where he defeated Tom Jenkins for the world's championship in freestyle wrestling.

Championship matches with profitable gates were only occasional events so Hackenschmidt, in the meantime, worked the English music halls for over twelve years. One of his friends, Norman Clark, recalled what life was like for the champion on the circuit:

Far from restricting himself to exhibitions with partners, he continued at all stages to take on all-comers. He had the sense always to keep his offers not monstrous, but just reasonable, and the public saw that the bouts he wrestled, if not always exhilirating, were, at any rate, usually genuine. He offered 25 pounds to any one who could stay fifteen minutes with him; 100 to any one who could put him down once; and 50 to any challenger who proved that he had failed to meet him within twenty-four hours of receipt of the challenge. Of course, it did not do to polish off every challenger as quickly as he could, and a certain number had to be allowed to get fairly close to the time limit before serious work was commenced on the champion's side. But even for the greatest champion such work has a considerable risk about it; a small wrestler on the defensive entirely can prove a very slippery customer, and in two or three cases the award for staying the requisite fifteen minutes was secured by challengers.[26]

It seems even in the early days of professional wrestling when genuine bouts could drag on for hours of dull defensive maneuvers and stand-off counterholds, the best of champions was not beyond using theatrics to please the crowd.

So it was in England at the turn of the century and soon after in America that the various styles employed in wrestling evolved into a fairly standardized professional format as international stars regularly met and tested each other's mettle. Some early greats chose to stay on the continent such as the Pole Otto Arco who triumphed at the Vienna tournament of 1903 and Gustav Fristensky, "The Bohemian Hercules," who won his first world's championship in Greco-Roman style that same year and his last at age 49 in 1929. But the majority of world-class competitors made it to England and some even journeyed to the United States. The German Arthur Saxon amazed the English with his feats of strength and held the world's title in belt wrestling from 1906 to 1909. Charles Vansittart, a wealthy French strongman who had visited the Klondike during the Gold Rush, was with Hackenschmidt that night at the Alhambra and stayed on as part of the champion's troupe. John Lemm, "The Swiss Hercules," won a 1908 tournament in London billed as the "Battle of the Giants." He defeated Ivan Padoubney of Russia, the former titleholder, Alex Cameron of Scotland, Matt Steadman of England, and two French contenders, Lamont de Beaucairois, and Apollon. Even the Great Gama of India came to Europe in 1910. His ability was so awesome that many wrestlers publicly avoided his challenge and would agree only to private club encounters with the master. In such a bout in England, Gama threw the very capable American Dr. Benjamin Roller 13 times in 15 minutes.

The point in citing all these names, dates and places is simple: by the early 1900s professional wrestling was an established international sport. That was long before most modern sports were organized into leagues capable of sustaining athletes as professionals and long before other professional sports could be called international in scope. Some of the troubles professional wrestling has today in being accepted as serious sport can be traced back to conditions surrounding its international development in the early years from about 1880 to 1910. The problems are similar to those noted above at the national level. There were international stars, each jealous of his reputation. There was a confusion of styles, rules, titles. Promotion was in the hands of individuals interested primarily in profits who had learned their trade in the theater. There were wrestlers who were also performers in music hall acts, plays and exhibitions of strength as well as being serious athletes. From the beginning the search for a clear, clean line between sport and show in professional wrestling is in vain, for there was none. The very success of wrestling in its early days stilted its maturation into a modern professional sport. It became atrophied as an athletic display or exhibition, a ritual game. Sports, rooted as they are in rite, stand apart from ordinary time and place and tend, therefore, to be conservative. Cynics may say the controlling interests cared only in preserving wrestling in a financially successful format, but many other factors contributed to making "pro rasslin," both at home and abroad, what it was and is.

All this is not to say the early wrestlers were performers rather than true athletes. Many prided themselves on their honesty in the ring, their wrestling ability, and the titles they earned; but their professional world extended beyond sport and reflected the mixed entertainments offered by the music hall and the vaudeville stage. The confused scene, however, did not prevent the early stars from earning public respect and honors. Muldoon, it was noted, became New York's first Commissioner of Boxing. Hackenschmidt, after over 2000 bouts with only two defeats, ended his career as physical education adviser to the British House of Lords. And Fristensky was given an estate in 1919 by Marsaryk to honor him at the birth of the nation as the outstanding Czech athlete.

Professional wrestling in the United States had entered into what was to be the first of many slumps in the 1890s—at the very time it was flourishing in Europe. Yet a recognized succession of matches produced a unified championship for several years. Martin "Farmer" Burns, an agile 170 pound contender, wrestled the title from the original "Strangler" Lewis in 1895. Two years later Burns lost the belt to Tom Jenkins, a one-eyed mill worker from Cleveland. Jenkins revived spectator interest in the sport as he displayed great skill and knowledge of holds in the style he preferred to call catch as catch can. For several years Jenkins reigned as champion. Meanwhile promoters once more gathered and trained troupes of four to six wrestlers who would take on all comers out on the summer fair circuits. Already in 1901 there was a looseknit organization of booking offices for the fairs. They kept the sport going and on the side recruited new blood into the game. In 1903 Jenkins accepted the challenge of a young contender, the Iowan Frank Gotch, who had been trained by Burns. Jenkins had no easy time in defeating his opponent who was quick, intelligent, tricky and extremely strong. Gotch won the second encounter in 1904 which prompted promoters from around the country to form the first loose organization for the sport, the National Wrestling Alliance. Jenkins was able to regain the title for a short time in a classic rematch in New York a year later, but then lost the title in freestyle that same year to Hackenschmidt who had come to these shores to clarify his world's title while touring the country. By 1908 the promotional network of booking offices, the NWA, had moved from the old rural fair circuit into the cities to expand operations to year-round matches that would draw on the large metropolitan public.

Hackenschmidt's hold on the freestyle title was shortlived, for several months after he defeated Jenkins he lost the belt to Frank Gotch in the first of two epic struggles. Gotch left the ring the champion in a match that will forever remain disputed. Hackenschmidt, a scientific perfectionist, claimed Gotch won by oiling his body to slip out of holds and greasing his hair with a turpentine pomade which he rubbed into the defending champion's eyes. In the great encounter of perfection and skill versus skill and trickery, trickery won. Gotch reigned until he retired undefeated as recognized champion in 1913. He had won a career total of 154 out of 160 matches, about half the number of bouts booked each year by an average star wrestler today. His title as freestyle champion of the world had legitimacy to it, for he met such international challengers as John Lemm, the European titleholder in 1908. Their 15 minute match ended in a draw. The brevity and the outcome of the bout indicate that there was concern even in those days not to have the various titleholders dethroned. The game already needed regional and local champions to survive in the many markets around the world. It also needed competitors who whould go all-out in short, timed matches rather than conserve their strength to endure a struggle of several hours' duration. Hackenschmidt did have one more chance at Gotch's title in 1911; but handicapped by a severe knee injury, he was unable to pin his nemesis who worked on the injury. The two Gotch-Hackenschidt battles exemplify the variety of tactics allowed and employed in early legitimate title matches. The gate for the great rematch in Chicago was an unbelievable $87,000. Hackenschmidt, at least, was consoled by his share of the profits plus his take from picture sales which amounted to nearly $30,000 more!

While the occasional championship bouts were seen as serious sporting events, even before the first World War "fans came to accept the buffoonery of matmen as part of an evening's hilarious entertainment."[27] In San Francisco, the west coast wrestling mecca, the first tag-team matches were introduced in 1901 to spice up the action. Much as today these were relay matches with quick trade-offs replacing the stalemate standoff then so common in legitimate matwork. It was in San Francisco, too, that attempts were made to regularize and upgrade the game. There the modern ring was first introduced; an 18 foot square padded mat was placed atop a resilient wooden base on risers. This ring gave the spectators a better view, but it also gave the wrestlers greater protection and added springy action to their acrobatics.

By the end of the first World War, there had been a quick succession of champions following Gotch's retirement. Then in the 1920s wrestling, like other sports, was invaded by an army of young men who had first learned sports in military training programs and by athletes who had graduated from intercollegiate competition. A new influx of European matmen also hit the American circuits, including Irish Dan O'Mahoney—master of the flying whip, the Turkish-born Ali Baba—a former U.S. Navy champion, Stan Zbyszko—doctor of laws, linguist and European champion, and later on Jim Londos—a classically built immigrant youth from Greece. Those who entered wrestling were intent on making money as promoters fed the ever-growing entertainment appetite of the public in the rambunctious, iconoclastic twenties. In this period interest in both amateur and professional sport grew in the nation as paying spectators began to support collegiate programs and professional leagues on a regular basis. The situation in amateur wrestling differed, however, from that in other sports such as baseball, football and basketball.

Amateur wrestling has always been primarily a participant sport even though paying crowds attend college meets in a few geographic areas. The transition from amateur wrestler or often college football player to professional wrestler is a change in nature or kind rather than simply a change in status and level of competition as in most sports. The amateur sport of wrestling in this country first emerged as an intraclub exercise in the New York area; there the first amateur championships were held in 1878 at the New York Athletic Club.[28] The sport was usually American folk-style or freestyle, a form of wrestling much influenced by the collar and elbow scuffling that came out of Vermont. Soon there were interclub meets and tournaments; by 1900 these were regularly being won by college men who had been working out in the gymnasiums built on campus for winter sports. Yale had held informal winter wrestling tournaments for years before its intramural squad challenged Columbia to exchange meets at the two schools in 1903. By 1905 Princeton and Penn had formed teams and joined the league for the first collegiate championships at Philadelphia. These were fairly loose experimental arrangements. With league growth, rules and regulations developed until Yale withdrew in 1911 because graduate students were no longer permitted to compete. Yet collegiate wrestling grew, and in 1916 the first New England

Conference Meet was held. The schools tried AAU rules that had evolved with club competition and established various weight classes along with a collegiate style which awarded points for control time and position of advantage in deciding the breakers. Early matches followed the prevailing professional model in that there were three periods of ten minutes each in a match.

Club wrestling and YMCA programs were bolstered by the AAU meets which had as one of their purposes finding talented athletes to mold into American teams for the new Olympics. The United States sent its first wrestling team in 1904 after getting freestyle accepted alongside Greco-Roman competition in the games. Steady growth is evident in the fact that before the 1924 Olympics, some 3000 entrants in freestyle gathered at 19 regional meets to select 150 qualifiers who competed at Madison Square Gardens in the finals. Most wrestlers were from colleges, some worked out of athletic clubs, and a few such as Russel Vis of Los Angeles had trained with professionals like John Pesek and Farmer Burns because there were no wrestling programs in their home towns. Squabbles between the AAU and the NCAA prompted college wrestling coaches under the leadership of Hugo Otopalik of Iowa State to set up their own annual national meets starting in the late 1920s.

Over the years even the pure participant amateur sport of wrestling has known displays of showmanship. When a powerful Oklahoma State team back in 1932 was on its way to an eastern meet, it stopped by little Washington and Jefferson College for a workout. The visit was intended to generate support for the fledgling wrestling program at the Pennsylvania college. When the Aggies paraded into the gymnasium decked out in cowboy outfits, they were startled to find a small crowd of 500 spectators dressed in tuxedos. The legendary coach Gallagher instructed his team members beforehand to take it easy in their matches by working through their ten minute bouts; anyone who pinned his opponent in less than five minutes would have to walk back to Oklahoma.[29] Giving the crowd what they want has not been limited to the professional game, it seems. The two basic approaches of coaches and wrestlers to their sport have evolved, wittingly or not, as attempts to enliven wrestling for spectator interest.

There are those who go all-out for a flashy quick pin, and there are others who keep quickly maneuvering about to gain points. Matches, it should be noted, have been artificially shortened to as little as seven minutes, and the point system has been refined to award offense over defense and evasion. None of these developments is inherently basic or natural to wrestling as the lengthy bouts in the Turkish tournaments and the legitimate championship matches of the past show. They have evolved, consciously or not, as attempts to increase the number of spectators at amateur wrestling meets and thus to insure continued support for the programs in school athletic budgets.

Many professional wrestlers, of course, have come from the amateur ranks. At the turn of the century Earl Caddock who started in YMCA programs in Iowa was one of the first. In 1909 he was given membership in the Chicago Athletic Club so that he could wear the club's colors in amateur meets. At the Panama-Pacific Exhibition Olympiad in 1913, Caddock won in three amateur classes, middleweight, light-heavy and heavyweight. He soon turned professional and finally in 1917 in a gruelling match beat Joe Stecher for the heavyweight title in two straight falls. The first took one hour and twenty-two minutes; the second lasted one hour, forty. Undoubtedly the skill Cadock had developed as an amateur in becoming the first "master of 1000 holds" served him well. Ed Don George from the University of Michigan failed to make weight in the light-heavyweight class while trying out for the 1928 Olympics. For practice he entered heavyweight competition where he surprisingly won falls over the favorite, Professor Roger Flanders of Oklahoma State. After the Olympics, George entered the professional ranks and won the title by defeating another former collegian, Gus Sonnenberg of Dartmouth, who had introduced the football flying tackle into the game.

When the Great Depression settled across the land, professional wrestling struggled to survive more as a diversion than as a serious sport. Collegiate football greats such as Ed George, Sonnerberg, Jim Browning with his airplane spin, and jumping Joe Savoldi of Notre Dame made good money entertaining the folk. Promoter Jack Pfeffer first introduced mud and cage matches and rediscovered the tag-team event. Women and midget matches added to the carnival atmosphere as people sought distraction and thrills at the expense of sport at wrestling matches. The press still covered cards but as entertainment rather than sport. The theater critic Paul Gallico looked back on the popular champion of the 1930s, the Greek Adonis Jim Londos, as a true classical tragedian in his matches.[30]

The new medium of radio was unkind to wrestling which is basically visual. While baseball and the rapid-fire routines of other sports were natural for radio, wrestling had nothing an announcer could handle. Costly travel expenses and fewer dollars for amusement hastened the splintering off of regional wrestling promotions, each with its own title claimants. The hard times encouraged older and poorer competitors to hang in the game longer and thus lower the overall quality of professional wrestling in the years through World War II.

The rebirth of the game after the war when wrestling met its medium in television is not the subject of this historical survey; that period merges with the present, the post-print visual world that has not yet become one global village. Wrestling metamorphosed after the war into a hybrid entertainment through television promotion of theatrical flout and flaunt. Though nobody admitted to watching it, everybody's kid brother, mother or grandmother—including Elizabeth II and Miz Lillian—became a follower of the game which numerically has grown into the most popular of international sporting entertainments today. The rest of this study examines aspects of this latest rebirth of wrestling, the oldest sport and ritual drama.

Notes

General information on wrestling which is non-controversial and has been passed along as common knowledge was gathered from works listed in the notes, original texts, and encyclopedias. It would be pedantic to cite all such sources when they are used. Notes have been given only to credit authors' original findings or controversial views. Naturally, we are endebted to many others; any errors in interpretation are our own. Our position is that of Huizingga who said so eloquently: "In treating of the general problems of culture one is constantly obliged to undertake predatory incursions into provinces not sufficiently explored by the raider himself" (foreword to *Homo ludens*; see note one immediately below).

[1]Johan Huizinga, *Homo ludens, a Study of the Play Element in Culture*

(Boston: Beacon, 1955), p. 1.

[2]Quoted by Angela Carter, "Giants' Playtime," *New Society* (29 January 1976), p. 228.

[3]Gregory Stone, "Wrestling—the Great American Passion Play," *Readings in the Sociology of Sport* (Univeristy of Toronto Press, 1972), p.302.

[4]As reported by Carl Diem, *Weltgeschichte des Sports,* Vol. 1 (Stuttgart: Cotta Verlag, 1971), p. 120.

[5]Norman Gardiner, *Athletics in the Ancient World* (Oxford: Clarendon Press, 1955 ed.), p. 28.

[6]Robert Yeager, *Seasons of Shame: The New Violence in Sports* (New York: McGraw-Hill, 1979), p. 128.

[7]*The Laws of Plato* (New York: Everyman Library, Dutton, 1960), pp. 178-9.

[8]R. Barsh, *How Did Sports Begin* (New York: David McKay, 1970), p. 398.

[9]This and the following quotation were translated and presented by Albert-M. Landry of the University of Montreal in a paper entitled "Synodal Legislation as a Source of Medieval Popular Culture" at the Popular Culture Convention in Chicago, 1976.

[10]Diem, *op. cit.,* p. 485.

[11]Calvin S. Brown, Jr., "Beowulf's Arm-Lock," *PMLA*, Vol. 55/3 (September 1940), pp. 621-27.

[12]Prolog to *Canterbury Tales*, line 548.

[13]Quoted by P. Cunningham and A. Mansfield, *English Costumes for Sports and Outdoor Recreation* (Great Britain: Barnes & Noble, 1969), p. 312.

[14]Diary entry for June 28, 1661.

[15]Foster R. Dulles, *America Learns to Play* (Gloucester: Peter Smith, 1963), p. 26.

[16]Reported by Mary N. Stannard, *Colonial Virginia* (Philadelphia, 1917), and quoted by Dulles, p. 34.

[17]Charles Wilson's book, *The Magnificent Scufflers* (Brattleboro: Stephen Greene Press, 1959) is an invaluable source for the history of American wrestling, especially the collar and elbow style. The reader should know, however, that Wilson passed along much inaccurate information on the general history of wrestling. The quotation is found on page 6.

[18]Wilson, *op. cit.,* p. 7.

[19]As quoted by Dale A. Somers, *The Rise of Sport in New Orleans, 1850-1950* (Baton Rouge: LSU Press, 1972), p. 168.

[20]Wilson, *op. cit.,* pp. 38-39.

[21]John Betts, *America's Sporting Heritage: 1850-1950* (Reading, MA: Addison-Wesley, 1974), p. 169.

[22]We are indebted for this analysis to a paper, "The Pagan Image in the Emergence of Mass Sport, 1875-1906," presented at the 1976 Popular Culture Convention in Chicago by Donald J. Mrozek of Kansas State University.

[23]It was Jahn, the founder of the Turners, who popularized the line: "Mens sana in corpore sano" from the Roman satirist Juvenal. This is a textbook example of quoting out of context, for Juvenal had actually said when viewing a strappling Roman athlete: "It is to be hoped that there's a sound mind in that sound body."

[24]From a book called *Jorrocks' Jaunts and Jollities 1831-34*, as quoted by Cunningham and Mansfield, *op. cit.,* p. 315.

[25]Walter Armstrong, *Fencing, Boxing, Wrestling* (London: Longmans

Green, 1893), p. 235.

[26]Norman Clark, *All in the Game* (London: Methuen, 1935), p. 123.

[27]Betts, *op. cit.,* p. 285.

[28]Most information on amateur wrestling has been gleaned from occasional articles written by Don Sayenga, the unofficial historian of the sport, for *Amateur Wrestling News.*

[29]Sayenga, *Amateur Wrestling News,* Vol. 21/3 (13 December 1975), p. 18.

[30]Paul Gallico, "That Was Acting," *Theatre News*, Vol. 33/1 (January 1949), p. 27.

Chapter Two

Sinew and Sequins:
Wrestling in the Age of Electronics

Men trifle with their business and their politics, but they never trifle with their games.

G. Bernard Shaw

The history of professional wrestling after World War II is first and foremost the chronicle of the game's relationship to the new medium of television. To understand the successful symbiosis of TV and wrestling, a recall of the technical reasons why wrestling had failed on radio is useful. Aside from objections that wrestling is not a true sport and thus not marketable on radio, wrestling presents nearly insurmountable problems for oral transmission. First of all, it is extremely difficult to describe wrestling holds and moves in words. It requires something approaching the conventions of a text on gross human anatomy to convey information accurately. There are approximately three hundred basic routines and up to one thousand terms for the estimated three thousand wrestling holds, moves and positions. Such a rich vocabulary would tax both the announcer and the audience. More importantly, however, wrestling differs radically from baseball, boxing, football and basketball which have all been highly successful on radio. All radio sports have logical story lines and are linear in time: they can be rendered or described in time, that is, in words. As the French sociologist and philosopher Roland Barthes observed: "A boxing-match is a story which is constructed before the eyes of the spectator; in wrestling, on the contrary, it is each moment which is intelligible, not the passage of time .... It demands an immediate reading of the juxtaposed meanings, so there is no need to connect time .... In other words, wrestling is a sum of spectacles, of which no single one is a function: each moment imposes the total knowledge of a passion which rises erect and

46

alone, without ever extending to the crowning moment of a result."[1] With the advent of television—the medium of the moment, the visual, the spectacle—wrestling came into the mainstream of American popular culture.

In the early days of live broadcast television, wrestling filled several immediate needs of the medium. Together with old films, orchestra concerts, comedy routines and boxing matches, wrestling helped block in the pressing need for regular program slots. For the viewers, professional wrestling is a crowd sport and may have had added appeal in the early days of television when relatives and neighbors gathered for the communal experience of an evening of TV watching. They could chatter and socialize while following the action on the little screen. As for the industry, production costs and fees for performers were low for live wrestling broadcasts. The game fit quite neatly into a television studio with floor cameras focused on a stage or ring that allowed close-up shots which were ideal on the six-inch home television screens of the day. Performers in the ring were recognizably human and not, as in team sports, antlike figures cavorting on a miniscule black-and-white playing field or court. Paralleling the Friday Night Fights, regular live wrestling shows were sent out by the television networks such as Dumont from the major broadcast cities of the day, Chicago and New York. (Live broadcasts and time zone differences made primetime productions from the west coast problematic.)

Weekly evening broadcasts of studio cards made wrestling stars, both heroes and villains, into nationally known personalities. The concentrated small-screen television set of the day stimulated wrestlers toward greater exaggeration, showmanship, histrionics and acrobatics. George Wagner, a trained psychiatrist and a good journeyman wrestler of the era, became a star people loved to hate when he assumed the prissy, marcelled villainous ring persona of Gorgeous George. Antonio Rocco, who was born in Italy and reared in Argentina, became the modern wrestling ethnic prototype as his agile aerial maneuvers thrilled millions and filled Italians and Hispanics with national pride. Television interviews between bouts gave wrestlers an opportunity to elaborate their ring personalities with histrionics and costume. The first masked matman had entered the ring in 1873 in Paris,[2] but early on television helped create the masked villain or hero as a standard feature of most cards. Another stereotype, the All-American boy—fresh from military service, college athletics or Olympic victory—gave a touch of sporting seriousness to the mat game as the hero's skill demonstrated American superiority to the delight of patriotic viewers in the days of the Cold War.

By the 1960s wrestling faded from network schedules and prime-time showing. A television set could now be found in every home, and TV had become a basic of life, not a curious novelty. For children, television was now their everyday companion; and many adults, too, found themselves addicted to the tube yet critical in their attitude toward the medium and its fare. The general viewing audience had tired of predictable weekly wrestling cards and third-rate punchers on the Friday fight cards much as people would grow weary if they attended a circus every week. The showmen promoters of wrestling whose live matches were still well attended quickly adjusted to the new reality of television. They had learned the tremendous advertising impact of the medium and developed a new TV format that proved mutually profitable to local stations and wrestling franchise holders. But as the sociologist Gregory Stone noted over a decade ago, promoters found that live matches could not be maintained without regularly televised matches in a market. And in the fringe areas of the television market, occasional live cards were necessary to sustain wrestling's televiewing ratings, regardless of losses at the gate.[3] Wrestling had become a parasite of television in what had in the 1950s been a symbiotic relationship between game and medium.

Wrestling on television has kept essentially the same viewing format for more than twenty years. Since the bouts, cards and stars are the subject matter of other chapters in this study, attention here is limited to technical aspects of the spectacle. For the typical television wrestling show, a promoter or franchise holder arranges taping of wrestling bouts at a local TV station. Tickets are issued so that fans will be present for needed crowd reaction during the two to three hour taping session usually held on a weekend so that preteens and families can attend. Care is taken that bouts will not exceed the ten-minute time slot between commercial interruptions on television.

Thus the local station gains a weekly show—usually an hour in length—to block into a programming slot outside prime hours such as Saturday or Sunday morning, or Saturday afternoon when other sports are slack or late evening. The station owner is assured a loyal viewership for lengthy mailorder and call-in television promotions and sales, plenty of time for required public-service announcements, and good spots for profitable local advertising of products and services such as used cars, hardware products and bars and restaurants that cater to the blue-collar public.

The advantage in this arrangement for the wrestling promoter is a blatant hour's commercial. The television card is one long promotion of the matches the cardmaker has booked in the near future at an arena in the viewing area. The TV wrestling formula differs from that used at live matches. Stars are to display their mat prowess. So the franchise owner retains a stable of weekend warriors, journeyman losers and young men learning the ropes to pit against class wrestlers on TV. The losers are clearly overmatched in these encounters. After a television match the winner, i.e., the star, is interviewed so that he can build up the "hype" for a coming bout he has against another hero or villain of star caliber on the next live area show. Very rarely do two name wrestlers meet on television. If they do, the confrontation ends as an inconclusive prelude to the "real" match on the coming arena card. Carefully orchestrated interference in a television bout or controlled mayhem during an interview are regularly added to stimulate maximum ticket sales for the showdown on the live card. An hour of televised wrestling often contains as much program time devoted to interviews and chatter about the big arena matches as it does actual wrestling action.

Advances in television such as light sensitive videotape and portable camera equipment have been used by promoters and stations in developing and marketing television wrestling. Camera operators can take clips of the action from the sports arena which are later worked into a television broadcast to build the fans' interest in a planned rematch at the stadium.

Interviews of stars taken on the road or in the lockerroom can be interspersed between the studio bouts. Matches from other areas of the country can be shown to enhance the arrival of a top wrestler who is about to join the alliance broadcasting the bouts. Stars with their busy road schedules can tape several interviews after a TV match to be packaged as needed for various opponents they are to meet in different markets on the alliance circuit. Thus even though a villain and a hero may be scheduled for several reruns of a classic feud in several cities, the local television station can air interviews in which fans are urged to come to the live match in their own hometown on a specific date. Also fewer local stations need be involved in the filming of television wrestling; all the taping of action and editing of interviews can be done in a studio in the hometown of the regional wrestling promoters. They then not only book the cards in other cities in their franchise territory but see to it that local TV stations receive appropriate videotapes to air prior to the live matches.

Studies have been conducted on arena audiences, and assumptions about viewers do determine advertising dollars. So far the impact of televised wrestling on children has remained an unresearched phenomenon though wrestling promoters have recognized the youth market. Every TV taping session has a large number of squealing and booing preteens in the audience. Wrestlers are not sports models for youngsters so much as they are live cartoon characters exaggerrating life as they struggle, menace, boast and wage a showy enactment of the eternal epic battle of good versus evil. The recent phenomenal appeal of Mr. T to children seems to validate this assumption. Older youngsters and teenagers are the group most interested in wrestling paraphernalia at live bouts, the group most prevalent at photograph signing sessions and in wrestlers' fan clubs. Promoters often cater to this public on television broadcasts by announcing that children are free when accompanied by a paid adult admission at the live matches. This is just good salesmanship because the children pester their parents into taking them to the matches. Also adults, who on their own might be hesitant to be seen attending wrestling matches, can indulge their curiosity or interest when accompanied by a child. Television wrestling announcers, too, inadvertently draw attention to the fact that the audience is composed in large part of impressionable young viewers when they warn that certain holds and maneuvers are dangerous and should not be attempted at home with friends. They certainly are not thinking of the proverbial grandmother who enjoys TV wrestling matches in the privacy of her home.

Given the local broadcast format of wrestling for more than a score of years, it is difficult to determine what public is watching and whether viewers might want more or would be satisfied with less. A poll conducted in 1978 gives some information.[4] Of the seventeen sports mentioned, professional football with 60% drew the largest following. Near the bottom of the list were skiing, swimming and wrestling—each had an audience of 4%; only track and field with 2% drew fewer. But when the same people were asked what sports they wanted to watch more on television, there were some unexpected results. Both major and minor team sports were about balanced off by those who wanted more and those who opted for less. Surprisingly, 12% wanted more professional wrestling on television; whereas, 16% could be content with less golf coverage. Obviously, any conclusions drawn regarding wrestling would be speculative. Promoters, the people who do determine the amount of television wrestling, seem nationwide in agreement that between two to three hours a week is just right even in very active markets with weekly live wrestling cards.

How wide a public has watched promotional matches on television over the years cannot be calculated, but the fact that "pro rasslin" has become a recognizable American icon suggests that the masses have been reached for over a generation. Cassius Clay, consciously mimicking the bravura of a wrestling heavy, transformed his considerable boxing talents into Muhammad Ali, a folk hero the public loved and hated. With this public persona, he revived interest in the moribund fight game during the 1960s. Filmmakers have followed Sylvester Stallone's lead back to the simple world of ring heroes. "Mad Bull" starring Alex Karras was a 1977 wrestling imitation of "Rocky." Then Stallone produced his own surrealistic image of the mat world in the 1977 film feature "Paradise Alley." A vintage Peter Falk film, "All the Marbles," soon followed; it featured a women's tag team with Falk as the manager. In "Rocky III," there was enacted the classic confrontation of boxer and wrestler as Rocky met Thunderlips, known as Hulk Hogan to wrestling fans. These and other films as well as episodes of television series such as "Starsky and Hutch," "Charlie's Angels," "The Fall Guy" and "Magnum P.I.," portray the matworld and assume common knowledge of wrestling as a folk icon that the public has gained from televised wrestling shows.

The spread of cable television to millions of homes and the break-through in satellite communications in the early 1980s found the entrepreneurs of wrestling among the first to use the new situation. While the format of TV wrestling has remained much the same in this third stage, the marketing has begun to change. For example, cable stations that are not network affiliates tend to carry wrestling on their program schedules more often than affiliated stations. Thus the sport reaches more markets than in the former stage of local promotional wrestling telecasts. Broadcast costs are among the lowest in the industry, and the promoter reaches more potential fans for his live cards throughout the region.

Some local promoters have expanded their territory to vast regional and even national markets. When Ted Turner's Atlanta station WTBS became via cable and satellite the first truly national station, "Georgia Championship Wrestling" broadcast Saturday and Sunday evenings suddenly became a weekly national show. Early on there was discussion about moving wrestling on WTBS from its Saturday primetime slot. That plan quickly died when WTBS's show swamped the TV wrestling competition on two other Georgia stations. Market analysis found the wrestling slot drew a viewership of over 500,000 in Atlanta alone and about 2.5 million of the 20 million cable homes were tuned in nationwide for a total estimated audience each week of four million. In the fall of 1982, "Georgia Championship Wrestling" was rechristened "World Championship Wrestling" to reflect the broader audience it attracts. The true sign of the impact of the cable broadcasts on the game of wrestling is seen in the fact that promoters in the alliance to which Atlanta belongs have bought up or killed off franchises in other wrestling areas and are moving their live shows onto what was traditionally others' turf such as Ohio and parts of Michigan. Gordon Solie, the Atlanta ring announcer, has become the Dean, the Walter Cronkite, of his peers. A veteran of more than twenty years in the business, Solie has mastered the art of understatement and deadpan essential as counterpoint to the hyperbole of the performers. Solie's weekly presence lends continuity to the show which would otherwise unravel into a chaotic parade of wrestlers engaged in verbal as well as ring conflict. Seeing Solie week after week reassures fans that all is well and ordered in the world of championship wrestling—if not in their own.

The USA entertainment cable network in 1982 carried "Southwest Championship Wrestling" out of San Antonio on Sunday mornings. The broadcast varied somewhat from the usual studio format discussed above. The Southwest show was taped the week before at a regular arena rather than in a TV studio. More importantly, the matches shown were real contests on the card. The combatants often were fairly evenly matched rather than obviously performing in promotions for an up-coming live card. There were the usual hype and interviews, but these all focused on coming television broadcasts while only secondarily serving for live cards within the immediate area. "Southwest Championship Wrestling" thus developed into something like a weekly wrestling television series for the nation.

Beginning in the fall of 1983 the USA network took a further step in bringing its weekly hour of wrestling into the television reality of the 1980s. Vince McMahon, Jr. of the WWF began hosting a show called "All American Wrestling" which replaced the Southwest broadcast on Sunday mornings. The McMahon show is a slick, careful imitation of the format used on weekly cable review shows in other sports such as football and basketball. Action highlights instead of whole matches from the various alliances around the country are aired. The result is a fast-paced hour of fairly good action of star versus star. While the interview feature is retained, only one matman is profiled each week. Gone is the old promotion for the next local card, and gone too are the reprehensible blood and gore displays.

The huge programming needs of around-the-clock cable

sports television means that peripheral and junk sports such as wrestling and karate have become a regular part of the program schedule. In addition to the wrestling shows on WTBS from Atlanta and the USA Sunday morning show, the USA Network has returned to the early days of television by scheduling a live professional wrestling card nearly every month from an eastern arena. The live card differs, as was described above, from the usual studio promotional videotaped matches. The bouts from the East resemble a boxing card on television. Of course, such broadcasts are used primarily to block in nights when major sports have light schedules or when the commercial networks have blockbuster programming. For instance, USA showed a live wrestling card opposite the Super Bowl in 1983 when it was obvious USA's share of the market would be miniscule.

Even the ESPN cable sports network has turned to wrestling in its search for more events to fill its twenty-four hour schedule. For the sports purist's network, however, only amateur wrestling is acceptable. NCAA wrestling tournaments have been shown in abbreviated version on ESPN. In December 1982, that network recognized wrestling as one of the fastest growing college and high-school sports when it broadcast its first Invitational College Wrestling Tournament from Caesar's Palace in Las Vegas.

Another recent development in the symbiosis of professional wrestling and television in the era of satellite broadcasting deserves note. Some independent promotions now tape promotional matches which are mailed or beamed directly to third-world markets such as island republics in the Caribbean. The videotapes are shown on local television to build up interest in wrestling and to establish star recognition. When the wrestlers finally arrive for a live card, they are welcomed as sports heroes and entertainment personalities. The card becomes a national event, a great spectacle, and a profitable venture.

*   *   *

Though television early along dropped professional wrestling from its sportsnews department, the medium has never outgrown the game. Typical of the official TV attitude is a quip by a sports reporter who showed a filmclip of a holiday mat extravaganza and added: "We don't have time to give you all the results of the wrestling show. We can report, though, that all who were supposed to win, did" (WCCO—CBS News, Minneapolis, Thanksgiving 1981). Yet professional wrestling, a prole spectacle, and the people's entertainment medium of television have continued an evolving, mutually profitable relationship.

The same cannot be said of the print media. City newspapers, the major promotional tool of regional sports, are vital for the support of hometown professional and amateur athletics. Day in, day out the local press devotes more pages to sports than to any other single interest in life. As manufacturers and sales personnel know, advertising aimed at males of all ages and classes will reach the widest market if printed on the sports pages of the local paper.

But as the readers of most newspapers know, professional wrestling very rarely receives any space on the sports page; it thus becomes a tacit non-sport. Coverage of the game is limited to an occasional captioned action photo or a human interest sketch by a local sports columnist. Some newspapers grudgingly carry the results of matches in scoreboard columns to save their sports departments a flood of nuisance calls from local TV wrestling fans who missed the live matches. Of course newspapers do welcome advertising announcing wrestling cards on their sports pages. But even then the matches often are listed as shows or exhibitions rather than as sporting events or contests, for laws in several states so stipulate; in Texas, professional wrestling officially comes under the predicate of burlesque!

An interesting parallel between professional wrestling in America and the bullfight in Spain has produced similar treatment by the press in each country. Spanish newspapers usually list bullfights under entertainment rather than sports. Actually, the "corrida" is poorly translated as bullfight; for it is an athletic, skillful ritual of dramatic tragedy. Bullfighting today is controlled by seven major promoters. They have let corridas become shows for uninitiated tourists who buy inflated tickets as Spaniards turn more and more to modern mass sports. Torreros nowadays are rarely in danger as they perform against slower, safer bulls. Both professional wrestling and the corrida have become ritual dramas that the press rightly lists under entertainments.

The treatment or better, ignoring of professional wrestling by the newspaper industry is ironic. For in a funny way, wrestling is the most honest business in a sports world which Howard Cosell once christened "the toyland of life." Wrestling thrives as an athletic entertainment in spite of being ostracized as fake by the official guardians and high priests of sport. The wrestling fraternity rarely reacts to its critics, for the old public secret that "pro rasslin" is a rigged show needs no more comment than would a play or a novel that a naive reviewer called a lie. Wrestlers who do respond are either evasive or disarmingly open. In an interview, a mat star of over thirty years quite candidly said of wrestling: "It's like the Harlem Globetrotters team. Matches are made according to how much money they can put in the house. The officials are part of it. But every sport is just show business. It's all showmanship. It's all entertainment. It's all television. It's all histrionics."[5] Only recently has the total sports industry—not just wrestling—been probed with an honest eye. Leonard Koppett, a former New York *Times* sportswriter, describes how the whole sports enterprise from owner and promoter to media coverage concentrates on creating and maintaining the fan's commitment to an illusion.[6] The fan's caring is ultimately the entertainment. The whole industry fosters in the fan a willing suspension of disbelief similar to that proper to a moviegoer or a novel reader. From this point of view, professional wrestling has been more honest than the major sports in America. Its top stars are not paraded as role models or heroes for children to admire. There are no drug and gambling scandals, no contract and legal squabbles in the wrestling game to fill sportscasters' broadcasts and reporters' columns. Wrestling remains what it has been since the days of Muldoon, an athletic diversion.

One type of local newspaper, the community weekly advertiser, does in some places carry a regular column on the local wrestling scene. Typical of such coverage is the tongue-in-cheek "Pro Wrestling Update" feature by John Sherman in the Sun Newspapers distributed in the metro area of Minneapolis and St. Paul. The blanket distribution, hometown chatter, and public service that characterize weekly advertisers makes them quite effective in getting the fans out to local matclubs. Frequent sellout crowds of over 18,000 at matches in the Twin Cites are due in part to Sherman's regular column in the *Sun Times Weekender*.

Major weekly and monthly publications, even those dedicated to sport, do not cover professional wrestling. What they do at times print is human interest stories on some of the more bizarre performers or treat the wrestling match as a pop-art phenomenon. Typical of the latter are "Friday Night at the Coliseum" in *Atlantic Monthly* of March 1972, and a *Playboy* photo feature in February 1982 of Andy Kaufman's wrestling spoof cum sex in which he declared himself the intergender champion of the world. Kaufman admitted that as a wrestling buff he perfected his flawless facades and caricatures by imitating the deadpan, straightforward role identification of many professional wrestlers. In his encounters in the ring and on the "David Letterman Show" with wrestler Jerry Lawler, Kaufman may have entered the twilight zone of wrestling reality. The public is left to wonder if they witnessed reality or spoof squared. A more serious tone is found in magazines when they feature human interest insights into wrestlers' lives. *Sports Illustrated* exemplified the respectful approach in a lengthy article simply entitled "Andre the Giant" in December 21, 1981. An article, "Wrestlers Jesse Ventura and Adrian Adonis Discover the Good Life as Bad Guys," in *People* of May 24, 1982, is an example of a magazine's attempt at a candid glimpse into the private and public lives of two temperamentally different grapplers.

Of course there are followers of wrestling marked by a singleminded or fanatic (whence, "fan") dedication to the game. For this public, there have been as many as seven pulp magazines on the national market at any given time during the past quarter century. Over the years there has been little change in these publications which are products of firms such as Dell which publish pulps on a great variety of special interests and hobbies. The wrestling monthlies have interchangeable names such as *Pro Wrestling, Wrestling World, The Wrestler, Wrestling Scene, Wrestling Revue*, etc.

Change of ownership is frequent; and though the names may vary as a result, the content and format remain much the same.

Wrestling pulps reflect the ambivalence in the business between sport and entertainment. Unlike most sports monthlies, the wrestling publication is instead more like the cult magazines aimed at avid fans of movie stars and pop-music performers. The wrestling monthly features interviews with leading matmen and reports on recent big cards. There are peeks into the private lives of some ring heroes and background reports aimed at fueling interest in current ring feuds. Nostalgia has its place in features recalling wrestlers of yesteryear and epic contests from the past. There is an obvious emphasis on photographs over words which is fitting for an athletic activity that is visual rather than textual. Common to most wrestling publications is a fan-club section where followers of the various stars or regional devotees find addresses of those of similar mind so they can exchange photographs and newsletters. A fair amount of the publication may then consist of material submitted by readers themselves; they send in photos and reports on results of matches in their towns, write letters to the editor, and take part in fan-club columns. Editors admit that articles in their magazines are often lifted verbatim from material originally worked up for programs sold at matches in the various franchise areas of the country.

Required in each wrestling magazine is a monthly rating list of champions and leading contenders in each of the three major American wrestling leagues (National Wrestling Alliance, World Wrestling Federation and the American Wrestling Association). Publications often are partial in their content covering one league more than the others. Some wrestling pulps contain reports on performers and matches from Europe, Japan and the South Pacific to give an international overview of the sport.

An aspect of the wrestling monthly that needs comment is advertising. As may be expected, there are ads for fan paraphernalia, Charles Atlas and self-defense courses, mailorder business schemes, sports books and home health remedies. For more than a decade as sexual explicitness has crept into all the media, many of the wrestling magazines have featured articles on female mud wrestling and so-called "apartment wrestling." Male mud and jello matches were gimmicks in the 1930s but have long been absent from wrestling cards sponsored by reputable promoters. It is true that strongwomen such as Minerva from Hoboken, New Jersey, were featured in publications in the naughty era of the old *Police Gazette* and that women's wrestling matches have been found on cards since the Depression days. The obvious sexual titillation was perhaps the main reason female wrestling was outlawed in many states, including New York, until recently. But official promotions and publications of the wrestling world in the past always treated women performers with the same straightfaced seriousness employed in discussing male wrestlers. New to the monthlies is the blatantly prurient appeal found now in many wrestling pulps. Increased sales to voyeurs is the motivation behind wrestling articles billed as "exotic sex." With the new content have come advertisers peddling books, photographs and video cassettes of fighting women; some even sell addresses where thrill seekers may pay to see what is euphemistically called "apartment wrestling." This all is a regression from the old days of *The Ring*, the "Bible of Boxing," and its spinoff publication, *The Ring's Wrestling*. Nat Fleischer and his successors at *The Ring* had intended publications of higher standards than the old *Police Gazette* which first covered the ring and mat games. The *Gazette*, because of its naughtier articles, was mostly circulated in the male citadels of yore— clubs, barbershops and bars. Up through 1981, *The Ring's Wrestling* still carried Fleischer's quaint claim to probity: "THE RING is a magazine a man may take home with him. He may leave it on his library table safe in the knowledge that it does not contain one line of matter either in text or the advertisements which would be offensive. The publisher of THE RING guards this reputation of his magazine jealously. It is entertaining and it is clean." Nat Fleischer, where are you today when the pubescent youths who buy the majority of wrestling pulps need you?

Genuine books about professional wrestling are rare, if not non-existent, because the two audiences that make the publication of sports books profitable are missing. First of all, there obviously is no market in wrestling for manuals on how to improve one's game as there is for most individual sports such as golf and tennis. Secondly, the acknowledged staging of the mat game prevents the development of living sports heroes and legends which is the other profitable market for publishers of sports books. At any given time, several manuals are available for interscholastic amateur wrestling as for any other athletic-program sport. But even in this regard the market is spotty, for amateur wrestling flourishes in limited areas across the nation and is as rare in some regions as ice hockey in the Sunbelt.

There are some anomalies within states, too. For instance, Oklahoma fields strong collegiate wrestling squads without local feeder high school programs. All this means there is a very limited public for books on wrestling of all types. Books on the oriental martial arts mark the contrast with the situation in wrestling most vividly. All reputable bookstores carry several titles on karate, judo, kendo, jujitsu, etc. as manuals for learning and improving personal performance, but few have one wrestling text in stock. In the category of sports heroes, there are no biographies of professional or amateur wrestlers available. But a leading American publisher was proud to risk a study of Jesse Kuhaulua of Hawaii who studied sumo and won the prestigious Nagoya Tournament in 1972 under his sumo name, Takamiyama.[7]

In recent years three books have featured professional wrestling, but none was from a major publisher. John Jesse's *Wrestling Physical Conditioning Encyclopedia* (Pasadena: Athletic Press, 1974) is basically a training manual on getting in shape and learning holds for amateurs, but it does contain an historical sketch of wrestling with photographs and interesting highlights on individual professional matmen over the years. Robert Morgan's *Main Event* (New York: Dial, 1979) is a gallery of grapplers for fans—glossies and biographical sketches—with brief essays on aspects of professional wrestling. These include the associations, the championships, the stars, the tag teams and the managers. An interesting old ring veteran and self-styled trainer, Champ Thomas, published through his vanity press a slim volume in 1976 called *Inside Pro Wrestling* as a complement to his handbooks on boxing. Thomas' book contains a glimpse behind the scenes plus a section on how to execute some professional holds and escapes.

The only other books that have devoted pages or chapters to professional wrestling in recent years have been sociological studies. Typical are passages in Don Atyeo's *Blood and Guts: Violence in Sports* (Paddington Press, 1979) and articles on the effect of wrestling on aggressive tendencies in spectators.[8] Wrestling as social situation was covered by the late sociologist Gregory Stone of the University of Minnesota for *Sport: Readings from a Sociological Perspective*,[9] and Thomas Henricks of the University of Chicago wrote on the dynamics of the wrestling scene in 1974 for *Sociological Inquiry* (Vol. 44/3). Two social scientists from the United States and Canada contributed an interesting comparison of role identification entitled "The Wrestler and the Physician: Identity Work-Up and Organizational Arrangements" to a study of the place sport occupies in the social order.[10] While amateur wrestling, rather than the professional mat world, is his interest, John Irving is the single current writer of note who probes the psyche of the wrestler with regularity in his novels such as *The 158-Pound Marriage* and *The World According to Garp*.

*   *   *

While young men take several routes to becoming professional wrestlers, their primary reason for entering the game is quite obvious: money. But the same could be said of most professional athletes today in an age when sport has lost its innocence. Participants no longer are players engaged in games but rather workers entertaining paying spectators. Crowd pleasing wrestlers on tight travel schedules can be booked for as many as six matches plus TV promotional bouts a week. Rick Flair, a major titleholder, was on airplanes 320 days in 1982. Such a hectic business pace easily means an income of well over $100,000 per annum for a top mat star. A few champions and international wrestling celebrities such as Hulk Hogan and Andre the Giant can earn $500,000 a year. That is gross income, however; for as in any small personal business, there are expenses to be deducted. Andre the Giant added up $67,000 spent on air travel alone one year while flying between 200,000 and 300,000 miles.

Most wrestlers today are recruited from the ranks of scholastic athletes; there are former football, hockey and baseball players, collegiate and Olympian wrestlers, and weightlifters too. Young men who have sufficient size and talent as athletes are at times directly approached by promoters who bluntly state there are great financial rewards in the game for a fellow who can make the grade. The straight-forward invitation is useful, for many young athletes hesitate to enter an athletic entertainment rather than a true professional sport. Scholastic stars are more eager to take up the wrestling game when they see they still have a chance at good money once they have been ignored or cut by recruiters from legitimate professional sports. Wrestling promoters and alliances are always on the lookout for new talent because their sport even more than others constantly needs new personalities. Sometimes franchises advertise for college athletes to come to training camps as was done in the spring of 1982 by the AWA in *The Minnesota Daily*, a university student newspaper.

Others enter professional wrestling because they come from families which, like circus and theatre families, have been in the game for a generation or more. The Howes may have been exceptional in hockey; but in the mat world, often father and son are both active performers at the same time. There are many father, son, uncle, and brother combinations in wrestling today. To name some of the better known, the von Erichs, the Gagnes, the Briscos, the Windhams, the Armstrongs, the Grahams, the Funks, the Hennigs, the Irwins and the Kiniskis. The game is a profitable business and is kept in the family.

Wrestlers regularly compete through their forties and into their fifties—sometimes even into their sixties. A typical star was Killer Kowalski who had begun wrestling on weekends while a student at the University of Detroit, first appearing on television in 1948. When he retired after thirty years in the sport, Kowalski calculated he had had an average of 175 matches a year and had wrestled in 47 states as well as Japan, Australia and South Africa. Some matmen enter the ring after retiring from football in their thirties and keep at their new trade for twenty years or more. Ernie Ladd is an excellent example of a wrestler who both played football and wrestled for years until he had to give up the gridiron but still could go on in the mat game. Verne Gagne was feted at age fifty-four in 1981 to a great retirement party after thirty-two years in the ring, but Gagne has wrestled on occasion since. Sixtime titleholder Lou Thesz, who won his first belt in 1937 and wrestled regularly for over fifty years, stepped once again into the ring in Japan in 1982. Longevity in the ring, however, is an old tradition. Stan Zbysko, doctor of laws and a wrestling titlewinner at age fifty-one in 1922, worked out at age seventy-six with Mike Mazurski for scenes in an English film, "Night and the City," released in 1950. Gagne's career is a good indicator of the profitability of wrestling for top stars as well as for longevity. He was drafted by the Chicago Bears and later given an offer by the 49ers in the early 1950s when professional football players were earning around $5000 a year, but by wrestling fulltime he was already earning between $25,000 and $30,000 a year. Bruno Sammartino's experience is similar. A career in football in the early 1960s would have guaranteed him $10,000 a year, but he already earned $30,000 to $40,000 in wrestling.

Of course not all who wrestle professionally are star material or stay in the sport for many years. And not all are even capable athletes. Promoters and franchise owners retain in their stables some second-rate weekend warriors, "good ol' boys," and assorted physical oddities. Depending on local taste, there are bleeders, behemoths, midgets, freaks, mama's boys, local school sports heroes beyond their prime and awkward musclemen. Some of these are kept on the books to serve as losers against stars—good and bad—in the television promotional matches and in preliminary bouts on live cards. But since the late 1960s, there has been a recognizable trend for professional wrestlers to be capable athletes trained in school and college sports rather than inept brawlers, clumsy big men, or prissy weepers.

Just how many active wrestlers there are at any given time is difficult to calculate. Live wrestling draws nearly fifty million admissions a year which makes it the third most popular spectator sport entertainment in America. The total of paid admissions alone would call for a great number of cards in a large number of arenas. *The Ring's Wrestling* magazine for October 1981 estimated there are more than twenty separate top wrestling cards with over one hundred individual matches in North America each and every day. So for promotions by allies of the three major wrestling alliances, more than two hundred wrestlers would be needed just to fill the daily bill of fare. For another perspective on the extent of professional wrestling, it is estimated that there are roughly five hundred arenas around the country which regularly book wrestling shows. In addition to the top cards with their attendant TV studio bouts, there are the matches of the independent or minor league wrestling promotions, of which there were approximately thirty-five organizations active in North America in 1982. Of course, not all wrestlers compete every day or even regularly. Some keep close to home base such as apprentice performers learning the trade, men with local business interests who enter the ring only occasionally in their home area, and the semi-retired. There are finally those American mat stars who frequently tour the Caribbean, Japan, the South Pacific and Europe. All these factors produce an estimate of about 2000 professional North American wrestlers active in the game at any given time.

The young wrestling recruit undergoes two stages in becoming a mat entertainer, for he must have both physical skill and crowd appeal. First of all, he either attends a training camp conducted by a wrestling association or he works out for an extended time with an established wrestler. Once he is physically ready for the ring, he begins the second phase of developing a marketable identity. In the first period, the professional wrestler's experience is similar to that of any novice professional athlete. The typical camp, which runs an average of ten weeks, trains recruits in the basic moves, feints, falls and holds of the mat sport. The veteran wrestlers conducting camp are rigorous and push the beginners to their utmost. The late Chris Taylor, for one, felt the pro wrestling camp he attended was physically more demanding than his Olympic training had been. By the end of camp, as many as two-thirds of the beginners have dropped out or been found not to be proper material.

The second stage of a wrestler's development can be rather tricky. He must work out his niche in the game by pleasing many people—the promoters and alliance, the established wrestlers on the circuit, and the public. Promoters sometimes put inexperienced matmen against old hands with years of ring expertise to help the youngster ease into the sport and become comfortable before a crowd—but also to test the novice's mettle. Established wrestlers at times are reluctant to meet new blood in the ring because inexperienced opponents can more easily cause injury. Also a newcomer may, in his zeal, inadvertently embarrass his opponent and thus discredit the local established pecking order. "Shooting" or straight wrestling is, of course, taboo in the professional mat sport. But there is concern that newer wrestlers or newcomers to a franchise may try to get ahead by discrediting their opponents. For this reason, alliances are known to keep competent wrestlers called "policemen" who in preliminary bouts weed out any rogue wrestlers before they might meet the local champion.

The toughest task, however, for the new wrestler is to begin to develop his ring persona or role. This is what will insure his survival in the game and can eventually lead to star billing with a comfortable income. Unlike other sport entertainers, the professional wrestler has to be his own public-relations expert. He himself must build up public interest—the hype; he must sell himself to the public through his ring personality and television interviews. How difficult this can be is suggested by the following rough statistics: of fifty to sixty agile skilled beginners in professional wrestling, only five or six remain with it any length of time; and of these, perhaps two eventually reach stardom and big dollars. The topic of role development is detailed elsewhere in this study. But as an aside here, it is interesting to note that wrestling good guys are reminders of the older, unambiguous, clean-cut heroes found in a less complicated, less cynical America. As the sociologist Orrin Klapp noted, such heroes are no longer looked up to as models in everyday life; they are considered "chumps." The modern U.S. hero can be worse than ordinary folk in various ways, such as personal morals. The villain, too, is often a complex, ambiguous individual today rather than the straightforward blackguard of a simpler era.[11]

Beside the inability to develop a successful ring personality, there are other factors which prompt a wrestler to leave the mat game. Injury is most obvious; all active wrestlers know physical pain and fear serious injuries that temporarily or permanently deprive them of work and income while adding up medical bills. But the very lifestyle of a successful entertainer—living out of a suitcase, constant travel, loss of privacy and maybe even personal life, frequent heckling or pestering by fans in public—discourage some wrestlers from continuing the sport. Laurent Souci, an Olympian hopeful in 1980 who became a journeyman professional, says he has no home point of reference. He is just in and out of one motel after another. Unlike other celebrities, wrestlers know their make-believe world does not carry over well into everyday life. Many were shy team players in college and find it hard to be in the limelight out of the ring acting out for fans what has been called a living cartoon role.

The major factor deciding if a wrestler survives, if he works or not, is his relationship to the wrestling establishment. As was noted in the first chapter, wrestling alliances in the United States grew out of the old theater booking office, burlesque house circuits of an earlier laissez-faire entertainment era. Thus wrestling antedates in its control structure most modern professional sports. For instance, wrestlers do not have agents, are not drafted and do not sign long term contracts. The performers are, in a sense, individual entrepreneurs selling themselves. On the other hand, professional wrestlers are completely subject to the owners, i.e. the promoters and regional alliances. Wrestling is a private business that remains jealously closed to all outsiders. As one anonymous matman wrote: "Wrestling is sort of a closed corporation. If you become part of it you will learn all the little tricks of the trade, but don't expect anyone to tell them to you to write about. There is too much money at stake. Wrestling is show business and very well run. They intend to keep it that way."[12]

In many states, the powers that control wrestling have quietly and successfully lobbied to keep their turf free of supervision by the athletic commissions. In fairness it should be said that membership on state ring commissions tends to consist mostly of boxing purists. Their interest in exercising control over professional wrestling seems limited to collecting annual license fees and a percentage (c. 4%) of the house at live matches in exchange for few discernable benefits to either the athletes or the public. How limited a benefit commission control is can be seen in a California regulation prohibiting athletes over fifty years of age from engaging in ring activity. This regulation prevented Lou Thesz from performing in the Bear State when he was still a championship holder. The wrestling alliances have never been able to stave off attempted probes by the U.S. Labor Department seeking information on the employment conditions of wrestlers.

The three major organizations in professional wrestling, American Wrestling Association (AWA), World Wrestling Federation (WWF), and National Wrestling Alliance (NWA) grew out of the regional arrangements and rivalries of the 1930s. There was a tacit recognition that their show business needed more cards booked and champions than one national hierarchy could provide. (There are as many as twelve national championships today.) As in legitimate sports, a market arose that was larger in geographic area and in public consumption of the product than could be satisfied by one league alone. The alliances today are headed by presidents or commissioners: Stanley Blackburn (AWA), Bob Geigel (NWA) and Vince McMahon (WWF). But the leagues they head resemble nothing else found today in American sport for profit. In organization, the alliances are characterized by tight control of corporate information, finances, production, and all workers in the trade. Unionization or declarations of athletes' rights are unheard of in professional wrestling. The occasional push and shove among the big three alliances for dominance suggests to the outsider a structural model most reminiscent of syndicate families. The thirty plus lesser wrestling alliances or leagues are either headed by up-start promoters trying to carve out a share of the market with lesser talent, or they are local promoters of long standing affiliated with one or other of the three major associations for the supply of mat talent. Fans get to know promoters from local television promotional bouts. As a lot, promoters tend to be folksy, shrewd businessmen on the lookout for talent they can develop into stars that will draw. Wrestlers complain occasionally about unimaginative, lazy promoters who let the tried-and-true wrestling formula earn income, recognition and tax write-offs for the promoters while they neglect furthering the careers of the wrestling performers and fail to increase the gate by innovation. But then that is nothing new in the old struggle between profit oriented theatrical producers and actors seeking stardom and lucrative engagements.

Most promoters, however, are alert to signing on wrestlers for matches that will build a continuous crescendo toward a never resolved mythic, ultimate showdown between good and evil. The heroes and villains come and go or switch roles, tag teams are formed of necessity and destroyed by perfidy, as the mat stars circuit ride and ticket sales go on. Vince McMahon, in talking about Andre the Giant, sketched the standard booking routine: "I saw right away that Andre needed to be booked into a place no more than a few times a year. Most of our men work one of our circuits for a while and then move to another. It keeps things fresh. A guy may work New England for a few months, for instance, go from there to the South and then on out to spend some time with Verne Gagne in Minneapolis. But Andre's different. The whole world is his circuit. By making his visits few and far between he never becomes commonplace.... The wrestlers and promoters all want him on their cards, because when the Giant comes, everyone makes more money."[13]

If classified information in the United States were as difficult to penetrate as the inner workings and the Trappist-like silence of the cognoscenti in professional wrestling, then the government and the CIA would have little to fear about national security leaks. Nevertheless, a rough outline of the working arrangements of professional wrestlers can be drawn from various conversations the author has had with grapplers over the years. Wrestlers are hired on by oral agreement to work an area for a set time—initially usually three months. A promoter, typically, guarantees the newcomer to his territory: "You will have matches." That means he will have a chance to develop a following in the region booked out of the franchise city. Wrestlers often sign contracts for specific matches but not general employment agreements. How individual matches are choreographed is described by the anonymous letter writer: "In the trade a match is discussed in terms of so many changes, or exchanges of holds. A promoter asks the wrestler for so many 'changes' for a given time. As to who wins—that depends on the local conditions. Whatever will draw the best crowd for next week will be the deciding factor. The wrestlers normally would not decide such matters. They are hired help."

The preliminary wrestler can have between three and six matches and perhaps a television spot a week; a real hustler who has arrived may perform in as many as eight to ten bouts, including TV, a week. Promoters thus exercise control and conformity by the number of bouts a wrestler gets—that is, the number of chances he gets to work. Pay at first is either a flat rate per week or a percentage of the live gate. There are unwritten breaking points in percentage pay between preliminary performers, semi-finalists, and main eventers. But since each man is dealt with individually, the wrestlers themselves are reluctant to tell one another how much they are earning. Top performers, contrary to the belief of many wrestlers themselves, do often have written contracts giving them a guaranteed income. But since most wrestlers rely on percentages and percentage bonuses, it is not uncommon at matches to see wrestlers in the wings checking the crowd so that they will not be scalped by the promoter when he pays them after the matches are over. The promoter's personal take of the gate runs about 20%.

Wrestlers are cowed by the threat of economic deprivation with fewer matches or no promoter willing to hire them if they talk too much or if they buck the system and its pecking order. The matmen know if they work hard by performing well, their pay will increase. Also many are reluctant to upset the established order because they get pleasure out of what they do—entertain appreciative crowds for good money. They do not wish to end their days in the minor leagues where both the money and the quality of fan attracted are poor. Given the conditions of their work, wrestlers often live an internal, loner or "in-group" life. They not only have business uncertainties to deal with, but also the discomfort of being entertainment figures who are constantly bothered or baited in public. The ring mask can be a safety device for ordinary life. On the positive side, many an arrived wrestler enjoys his freedom to move about the country, to earn good money to invest in a second business and the daytime hours he can spend with his family when he is working out of a given city. Many clever, financially provident wrestlers such as Verne Gagne and Ole Anderson gradually end their mat careers working more and more at the business side of the game as road managers, promoters or even owners of a wrestling franchise.

As long as the majority of North Americans remain indifferent to the one world-cup sport, soccer, there are only the Olympics and the two tarnished ring games of boxing and wrestling as international mass sports for Americans. There is ironic humor in the fact that professional wrestling is more truly an international sporting activity than are the major U.S. professional sports for all their Super Bowls, World Series, and All-Star Games. As was noted above, wrestling was well established as an international spectator entertainment in the days of the great European tournaments at the turn of the century. Those early meets set the format followed in most pro-wrestling on the European Continent today.

Professional wrestling there tends to be a seasonal happening like an annual fair. Cities such as Vienna, Bremen, Hamburg, and many others have tournaments each year of two to six weeks in length. The individual cities set their tournament dates so that many wrestlers move on an informal circuit from town to town. For example, Austrian tournaments are held in the summer while major German shows are booked in the fall and terminate before the holidays. At a tournament, the fifteen or more participating wrestlers from many countries including the U.S. enter the ring daily for six nights running; then the matches of the evening are announced. Every day fans are treated to five or six matches with one often a tag-team contest. In working toward determining a champion, all contestants eventually meet each other in theoretical round-robin elimination on a point system. Actually, little attention is paid to points with wrestlers joining and leaving the competition as the show progresses toward the final days.

Continental professional wrestling, which is officially

called an athletic performance rather than a sport, differs from the American version in several ways. First of all, there is no television broadcasting of pro wrestling. Posters around town and newspaper advertisements plus the annual tournament tradition assure the promoter a public. Strict ordinances against children witnessing violence on television, in movies, and other entertainments prevent youngsters under age sixteen from attending the matches. So the audience is different than in the United States, but still it is composed mostly of youthful workingclass people.

The basic holds, escapes, and routines are much the same as in North America though most bouts are on the round system. Matches consist of five rounds of four minutes of action with one minute rests between. A man loses by pinfall or conceding. Knockdowns are counted as in boxing, the aggressor may not pounce on an opponent downed by a blow. But if a man is brought to the mat by a wrestling hold, then ground work continues. The round system with knockdowns and rest periods promotes heavy blows and fast continuous action. In some bouts, winners are determined by the number of knockdowns alone. Referees tend to be more on top of the action in Europe than in the U.S. There are many warnings and fines issued by the referee. But in Europe, too, the biased, corrupt ring official is a common character in the plot who adds to the suffering of heroes and the amusement or consternation of the crowd. Results of matches remain as inconclusive and predictable as in America. About one third of the contests go the time limit, one third end in disqualification, and the rest see one man pinned or conceding the match. The stars and champions win with predictable regularity.

The wrestlers themselves are often seasonal workers who have other businesses or are circuitriders traveling about Great Britain, the Continent, the Near East, and even Africa as they follow the tournaments. Some eventually make their way to North American alliances such as the Englishman Billy Robinson and the Austrian Otto Wanz, who held the AWA championship for a few months in 1982. In exchange some Americans including Nick Bockwinkel and Brad Rheingans take part in European meets. But for the most part, the working situation of European stars is not as comfortable as that of their American counterparts. There are fewer opportunities for young men to make their way to professional sport in Europe than in America. No scholastic sports programs exist, and soccer is the only well established professional sport. So wrestlers come either from amateur soccer, the Olympics, through family tradition, or via contacts with the promoters. Tournament wrestlers are housed either in cheap hotels or in trailer homes. They are paid on a per diem basis and must cover their own expenses. If the tournament is held outdoors and matches are cancelled by the weather, the wrestlers receive only one third their daily wage. Promoters' economic control and the trade secrecy are as tight as in North America.

Some national differences do exist. In Great Britain, for instance, professional wrestling has been a favorite show on television for years. There the tradition of varied weight classes has con⁺inued as in boxing. Speedy smaller men put on thrilling aerial shows for faithful followers alongside the more ponderous heavyweights. Also the British have regular weekly or monthly matches as in North America rather than tournaments only. Matches are booked, on occasion, in prestigious arenas such as Albert Hall and have in the past even been patronized by royalty including Prince Philip.

The game as practiced in the South Pacific areas of Australia, New Zealand, and the islands is essentially the same as wrestling in North America. There has been communication over the years between the two geographic areas—witness the name Australian tag-team match (which had nothing to do with Australia). Wrestlers such as the Kangaroos and Tony Garea from Down Under as well as Samoans and other islanders have become regulars on American mats, and many Yanks have toured the South Pacific.

Japan is another hotbed of modern professional wrestling. There are two contributing factors to the phenomenal success of the game in Japan. The first is the well known trend of the Japanese to assimilate, adapt, and even perfect things American following World War II, from baseball to manufacturing techniques to Santa Claus. Japanese television, as American TV before it, naturally found the dramatic agonia of wrestling fitting fare. Along with TV came live matches. The Japanese, who knew an aristocratic closed martial-arts tradition, also had the continuous tradition from antiquity of professional wrestling in sumo; and that was the second factor. Even today grand champions in sumo are national heroes such as the great Taiho who competed from the late 1950s until 1971. His record of 872 wins, 32 Emperor's Cups—six of these in succession and eight perfect tournaments—are national sporting statistics comparable to the data sheet on an American baseball great. The Japanese public was primed by sumo for the complementary prole diversion of wrestling American style and quickly took to the game.

Today, many Japanese stars tour the U.S. mat alliances as North American grapplers visit the Orient. The American follower of professional wrestling recognizes some of the impact sumo and the martial arts have had on the professional mat game. Japanese professionals who come to America are usually men of great bulk but very skilled competitors; they work up the crowd by incorporating some sumo ritual along with techniques from the martial arts. In defense of the stereotyping of Japanese matmen as sneaky, it is worth noting that American wrestlers are at times the villainous ethnic heavies when they perform in Japanese rings. It was evident that professional wrestling had arrived big in Japan when the world press helped build the tension surrounding the latest boxer versus wrestler farce in 1976. With a guarantee of $6,000,000 from Japanese promoters, Muhammed Ali met the Japanese wrestling titleholder, Antonio Inoki, in an embarrassing closed-circuit TV anticlimax broadcast around the world.

It is tautology to state that the entertaining ritual and spectacle of professional wrestling depends ultimately for survival upon followers, spectators, fans. Those involved in the business side of the game, however, often treat their public with little more than P. T. Barnum cynicism. The defensiveness surrounding pro wrestling prevents the in-group from being open or available to the public. Though not intended, the very wariness and unavailability of wrestlers away from the ring add to the mystique and ritual drama of the mat action. The recurrent assertion that wrestling is fake prompts cautious defensiveness on the part of the performers. The standard evasion by wrestlers is to cite their injuries as evidence of the reality of the action and to invite the dubious into the ring. Typical is the litany of woes by George Kidd, a former British light-weight champion: "I have two cauliflower ears and I'm deaf in one of them. I've had broken ribs, a broken nose and have a torn tendon which makes one calf permanently smaller than the other. Wrestling can kill a man. And has on two or three occasions. It's the constant pounding rather than the one bad fall that does the damage."[15] Whether fans believe in the "reality" of the action or not is beside the point. (Studies suggest they do not, on the whole). Perhaps the best illustration of the typical fan's attitude was expressed by a lone star patron glued to the action of a TV wrestling match who was heard to shout: "I don't give a damn if it is a fake! Kill the son-of-a-bitch!"[16]

It was noted that a wrestler must please many people in order to survive in the game. But be he contemptuous or appreciative of his followers, it is they who make him an entertainment personality and financial success. Some such as Bruno Sammartino admit it is fan support that keeps them at the trade when they are over worked, tired and hurt. Other wrestlers actually relish their star, their TV celebrity status. Some enjoy the excitement fans generate. As one wrestler expressed it: "Energy at a wrestling match generates ten rows out—not at ringside—and extends out into the balcony and back toward the ring. Wrestlers and audience are part of the same experience and act. You can actually hear the building play, up and down. You realize what you're doing—entertaining people, and so there's a sense of accomplishment after a match."

On the other hand, many wrestlers who perfect villainous personae that bait fans for the sake of large incomes become cynical and develop an attitude bordering on contempt for the followers of the game. A team of bad guys are blunt in expressing their jaded view of the fans they manipulate. Jesse Ventura admits: "We need the fans, but that don't mean I gotta like 'em. I've grown a great dislike for 'em." His partner, Adrian Adonis, elaborates: "Money's tight. People need to take out their frustrations. The American people are sickos who love violence and the sight of blood."[17]

There are, though, wrestlers who recognize their responsibility and that of the promotions for the behavior of fans. As one said in disgust: "The formula has become unredeemable, indefensible, blood." Another added that wrestlers themselves can improve the image of their sport by staying in shape and backing the hoopla with genuine athletic ability rather than resorting to chain matches and other sickening bloodsport spectacles.

Elsewhere this study examines the role of fans as audience. Here it only need be noted that despite all the studies of current wrestling fans—as to their reputed lower socio-economic status, their need for mass catharsis and release of frustration—that wrestling as a spectator entertainment is as old as civilization. Fan clubs, matches at polka festivals or rodeos, cookouts for fans at a mat hero's ranch are but current manifestations of a folksy human delight in game and spectacle. The wrestler unlike other sports figures is still human, individual and intimate. He is not a distant insect size creature on a field encased in a uniform, distinguished only by position and number. His face is known from television; he physically passes through the crowd on his way to the ring; there is still handshaking and verbal interaction possible between spectator and actor.

For those who find no redemption in modern professional wrestling, the semiotician and novelist Umbreto Eco offers a thought that can be applied to the game:

> Is it not also natural that the cultured person who in moments of intellectual tension seeks a stimulus in an action painting or in a piece of serial music should in moments of relaxation and escape (healthy and indispensable) tend toward triumphant infantile laziness and turn to the consumer product for pacification in an orgy of redundance?
>
> . . .
>
> As soon as we consider the problem from this angle, we are tempted to show more indulgence toward escape entertainments, reproving ourselves for having exercised an acid moralism on what is innocuous and perhaps even beneficial.[13]

The human chess of wrestling—the only sport attributed to God in that mystic encounter with Jacob, advocated by the philosopher Plato, enjoyed by Japanese emperors of yore and medieval kings, and practiced by Presidents Washington and Lincoln—will survive the excesses of promoters, grapplers, fans, and sociologists in our day.

Notes

[1] Roland Barthes, *Mythologies* (New York: Hill and Wang, 1972), p. 16.

[2] Roberta Morgan, *Main Event* (New York: Dial Press, 1979), p. 134.

[3] Gregory Stone, "Wrestling—The Great American Passion Play" in *Sport: Readings from a Sociological Perspective,* Eric Dunning, ed. (Toronto: University of Toronto Press, 1972), p. 312.

[4] Poll conducted by Opinion Research Corporation and reported by Don Kowet in *TV Guide* of August 1978, 19-25.

[5] Killer Kowalski as quoted in a wire-service interview, "Shutterbug Shudders at No One," carried by the *Duluth News-Tribune,* February 5, 1978.

[6] Leonard Koppett, *Sport Illusion—Sports Reality* (Boston: Houghton-Mifflin, 1981).

[7] John Wheeler, *Takamiyama, The World of Sumo* (New York: Harper & Row, 1973).

[8] John M. Kingsmore, "The Effect of a Professional Wrestling and a Professional Basketball Contest upon the Agressive Tendencies of Spectators," in *Second International Psychology of Sports,* Symposium, G.S. Kenyon, ed. (Chicago: Athletic Institute, 1970), pp. 311-316.

[9] Stone, *op. cit.*—see note 3 above.

[10] M. Michael Rosenberg and Allen Turowetz for *Sport and Social Order,* D. W. Bell and J. W. Loy, eds. (Reading, Mass.: Addison-Wesley Publishing Co., 1975), pp. 563-574.

[11] Orrin Klapp, *Heroes, Villains, and Fools: The Changing American Character* (Englewood Cliffs: Prentice-Hall, 1962), pp. 174 ff.

[12] As quoted by Stone, *op. cit.,* from a letter written in 1965, p. 310.

[13] As quoted in "Andre the Giant," *Sports Illustrated,* Dec. 21, 1981, p. 82.

[14] As quoted by Stone, *op. cit.,* p. 318.

[15] As quoted by Don Atyeo, *Blood and Guts: Violence in Sports* (Paddington Press, 1979), p. 163.

[16] Stone, *op. cit.,* p. 301.

[17] As quoted in *People* magazine for May 24, 1982, p. 89.

[18] Umberto Eco, *The Role of the Reader* (Bloomington: Indiana University Press, 1979), p. 121.

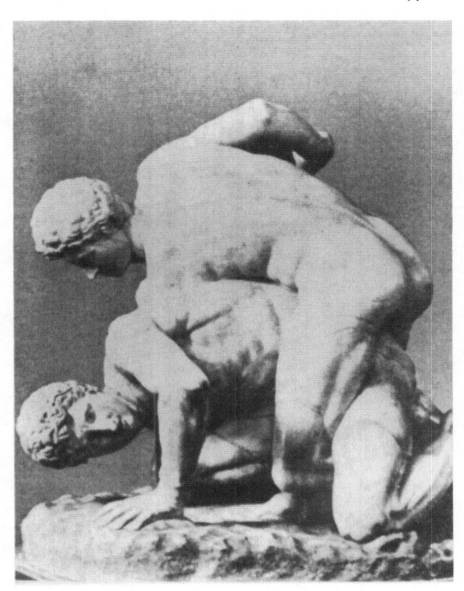

Classical sculpture
"The Wrestlers"

Meister Ott's "Art of Wrestling" from the year 1443

Meister Ott's "Art of Wrestling" from the year 1443

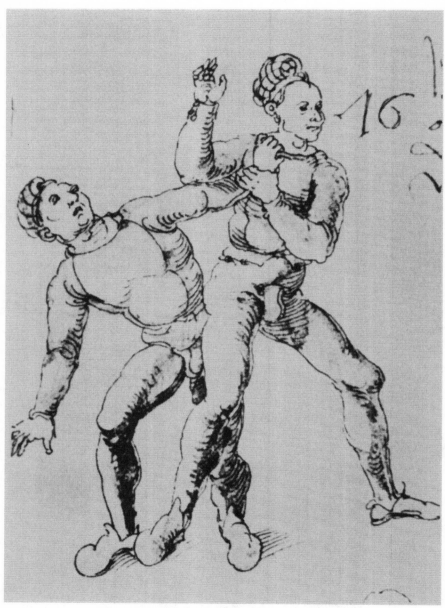

Wrestling manual from Dürer's school c. 1512

Wrestling manual from Dürer's school c. 1512

Wrestling manual from Dürer's school c. 1512

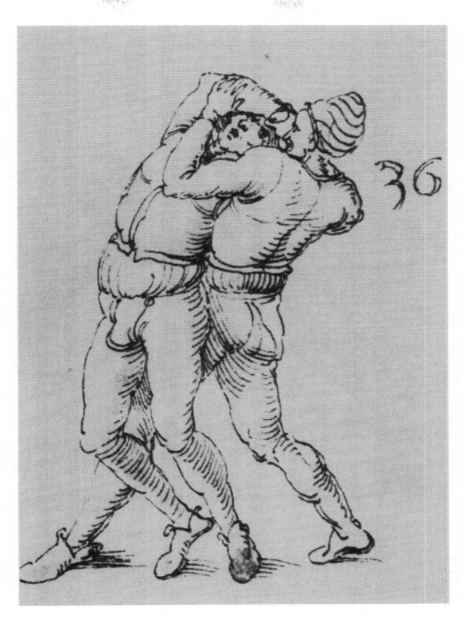

Wrestling manual from Dürer's School c. 1512

84

Fabian von Auerswald's "Wrestler's Art" 1539

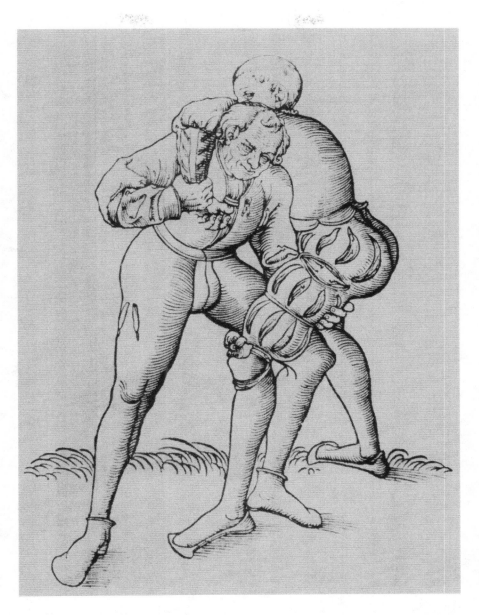

Fabian von Auerswald's "Wrestlers' Art" 1539

Nicolaes Petter's "Self Defense" 1674

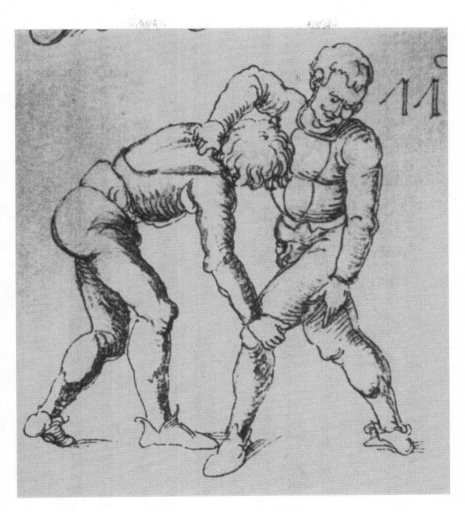

Wrestling manual from Dürer's school c. 1512

Wrestling manual from Dürer's school c. 1512

Turn-of-the-century postcard from an international tournament

Turn-of-the-century postcard from an international tournament

Japanese Champion Antonio Inoki in action against an American star

Bill Muldoon in his prime

Recent U.S. collegiate match

Capsules and razor nicks are commonly used to give the appearance that a wrestler has been injured enough to bleed. Here, despite a wound on the forehead, Bob Armstrong continues to stomp his adversary Ron Fuller.

Championship belts and over-dressed managers are an essential part of wrestling. Pictured (left to right): Arn Anderson, Billy Spears, and Jerry Stubbs.

One variation on the wrestling theme is the pole match in which the object is to climb a pole in one corner of the ring to a waiting purse for the winner.

Most evening's cards will have at least one match in which a wrestler will enter the ring with a folding chair carelessly left unattended at the edge of the ring. Such brawls are the stuff of which modern professional wrestling is made.

At seven feet and five hundred pounds, Andre the Giant is without a doubt the sensation of the wrestling world. Here he towers over the fans entering the ring in Montgomery, Alabama.

Ever since Georgeous George and his valet Jeffrey, wrestlers have been accompanied by various ring attendants. Here Rip Rogers is followed by his valet Brenda Briton.

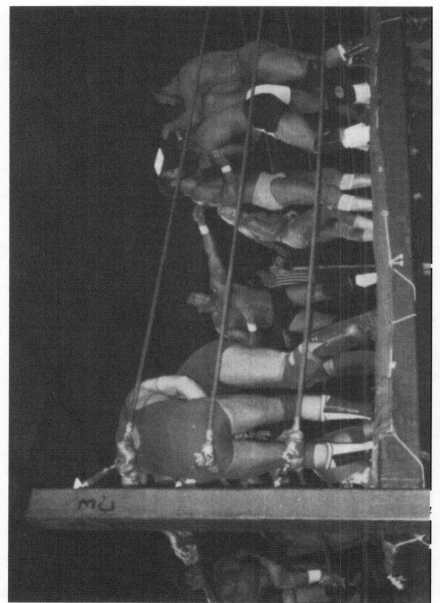

A common crowd pleaser, the battle royal begins with a ring full of wrestlers. When a wrestler is thrown over the top rope he is eliminated. The last wrestler in the ring wins the purse.

Very few wrestling matches are completely conducted within the confines of the ring. Here Scott Armstrong batters Arn Anderson before a match...

...leaving him unconscious and attended by his partner.

Chapter Three

Professional Wrestling's
Roots in Theatrical Traditions

Duke Frederick: You shall try but one fall.
Charles: No, I warrant your Grace you shall not entreat him to a
second that have so mightily persuaded him from a first.
Orlando: You mean to mock me after. You should not have mocked
me before. But come your ways.
Rosalind: Now Hercules be thy speed, young man!
Celia: I would I were invisible, to catch the strong fellow by the leg.

As You Like It, Act I, ii, 186-194.

In 1978 I was sitting in the Knoxville, Tennessee Civic Coliseum watching a rather boring preliminary wrestling match between Tony Peters and another wrestler whose name completely evades me when, after a particularly poorly performed maneuver that left both Tony and his opponent sprawled out in the center of the ring like turtles on their backs, a man a few seats away from me shouted rather fiercely, "You better practice that one some more before you try it again!" His statement reveals a number of important assumptions he had made about what was taking place in front of him and what he had in fact come to see, his obvious frustration being based upon his not getting what he felt he deserved for his five dollars. First, he was acknowledging that the match was in fact a performance that not only could but also should be perfected during rehearsals.[1] Second, he was casting the wrestlers in the roles of actors who were responsible to him for the performance they gave. Both points are basically concessions that wrestling fans are willing to make. But the third notion, and definitely the most significant one, came to me later and only after hearing the same man comment on how dangerous would be the match that was about to pit Bob Roop and Bobby Orton, Jr. against Kevin Sullivan and Dean Ho, the

103

Southeast Heavyweight Tag Team Championship being at stake. Obviously, the man was there because he wanted to believe, even if for only a few hours, that the performance was an actual competition. Yet, his first comment reveals that he knew better and that he resented a poor job that broke the illusion for him as had the first match of the evening.

The final event of the same night's card was a special treat for the fans as Professor Boris Malenko had agreed to wrestle whatever Ronnie Gravin had in his box—described by Garvin as something that would "claw, scratch and kill a man"—if Garvin would then defend his Southeast Heavyweight Championship Belt in a match against Malenko. What followed had the basic characteristics of spectacle. Garvin entered the arena riding atop a massive wooden box that was being carried to the ring by a forklift. After arriving at the edge of the ring, Garvin hurled a few insults before opening the box, out of which jumped five lovely lady wrestlers who presented Malenko with a bouquet of roses before pouncing on him with the fury of rabid dogs. Quite incidentally, Garvin jumped into the ring at an opportune moment and pinned Malenko. Not much of a wrestling match, but the audience loved it, including the man sitting near me who kept pointing out that it was just what Malenko deserved. Indeed, my companion for the night's matches wrote in his weekly newspaper column about the whole evening that it was the "best show in town for the money."[2]

All this points up what is often said but seldom really understood about professional wrestling, that it is a show rather than an athletic competition. This assessment is, of course, quite true as far as it goes. Wrestling is, however, a show that borrows from a number of well-established theatrical traditions, not a haphazard effort to fool the audience. More specifically, professional wrestling has elements of the morality play, allegory, the Noh Drama, and the classical theatre. The purpose of this chapter is to discuss how professional wrestling makes use of these various theatrical traditions and what it borrows from each. I will, in a later chapter, discuss why despite this fact wrestling cannot be appropriately referred to as theatre.

If one were doing a review of a Broadway premier,

legitimate responses might well center on scenery, character, costuming, staging, and conflict or action. Most of these elements of theatre, moreover, are equally significant for one's response to a professional wrestling match. While scenery is to a large extent an inappropriate concern, as it would have been to any preRestoration reviewer, much of professional wrestling's success pivots on careful orchestration of the other four. Chapter four will deal in depth with character; it is sufficient to say here that every professional wrestler assumes some character role, and his success is measurable in large part by how effectively he plays that role. There are, moreover, leading and supporting roles, all structured to support a larger design than offered by an individual match. Each match is but a vignette in the on-going drama of the ring based on a script something like that of a daily soap opera episode. Costuming, likewise, is essential to role identification, for the characters that wrestlers assume are highly stylized; thus the costume becomes symbolic of how the wrestler will act in the ring based on the role he will play. Staging, too, is fundamental to the success of professional wrestling. There are approximately twelve basic patterns according to which a match can be choreographed, with another twelve or so types of matches that can employ these patterns. For example, a match can go to the hero or the villain by pin fall, through the help of outside interference, by disqualification, and so on. The match can take place in a cage, with the wrestlers strapped to each other, or with other wrestlers stationed around the ring to prevent a competitor from running if the going gets tough. All told, there are approximately one hundred and forty-four basic variations on the general theme that the script can follow in the staging of a match. The theme is the conflict of good and evil although there is occasionally a match between two "good guys" that treats the fans to a "scientific" match or a bout between two "villains" that, even better, offers a blood orgy. These basic principles of theatre are consciously used, not the result of coincidence. To see this fact, however, we should now turn our attention to various theatre traditions and see how closely they are paralleled in the ring.

In "Professional Wrestling as Moral Order," Professor Hendricks, in one of the few scholarly attempts to deal with the phenomenon of professional wrestling, describes the sport as an "exaggerated morality play fervently manipulating the prejudices of its audience as quickly as it could perceive them."[3] Hendricks' qualification "exaggerated" is quite to the point and extended by Leo Rothsten's observation, "No morality play ever had such mighty heroes, such monstrous villains."[4] While Professor Hendricks' point is well taken, Rothsten's is perhaps guilty of journalistic hyperbole. Yet, both writers clearly point up the relationship between professional wrestling and the morality play tradition as it is generally noted in articles written about the sport. Just as a morality play dramatizes conflict between abstract virtues and vices, the basic conflict of professional wrestling is between good and evil, depending upon the current generation and what they see as being good and evil. This relativity accounts for the second part of Hendricks' comment about the manipulation of prejudices.

The scholar of dramatic literature A. H. Tolman has described two basic types of morality play, the "full scope" morality play that deals more generally and more abstractly with the theme of saving man's soul and the "limited scope" morality play that deals more specifically with this theme by dramatizing a particular moral dilemma or conflict between good and evil.[5] Talking about professional wrestling in general the first of these distinctions would be helpful. Our concern with specific matches, or vignettes, would demand that we call upon the latter. Generally speaking, the conflict between two wrestlers, perhaps resulting in a long series of matches before the outcome can be determined, does take on a symbolic nature, limited in scope to one manifestation of good combating one manifestation of evil. The nature of good and evil, as Professor Hendricks suggests, is dictated by the attitudes or prejudices of the audience and will change in accord with these attitudes and prejudices. For example, a recent ring war in Georgia involved Tommy "Wildfire" Rich and the Masked Superstar. Even a novice watching his first match would quickly recognize Rich as the hero and the Masked Superstar as the villain. If the mask were not enough, as it no longer is as numerous masked wrestlers are seen as heroes, to identify the Masked Superstar as the villain, Tommy's shoulder length blond hair and boyish good looks would be a giveaway that he is in every sense the embodiment of clean-living American youth. The conflict between Rich and the Superstar took on the dimension of good versus evil in a general sense because while Tommy, like Beowulf fighting the dragon, was willing to get into the ring and battle his adversary, accepting whatever fate head-on competition delivered,he was constantly faced with the Superstar's willingness to take whatever assistance a fellow villain would offer from outside the ring. Theirs was a brutal feud, basically begun when Tor Kamata and Ray Stevens entered a steel cage that surrounded the ring and helped the Superstar beat Rich without mercy. They left the hero unconscious and lacerated, his nose broken and his face bloody. Evil, however, did not win out, for the Superstar was suspended from wrestling for a time, thus finding it necessary to get revenge by placing a ten thousand dollar bounty on Rich's head to go to any wrestler who could finally end his wrestling career. No one succeeded, although many tried and were themselves made to suffer at Rich's hands, including the Superstar who simply changed masks and began wrestling as the Masked Destroyer. All during the supposed suspension, Rich demanded that the Superstar be allowed to wrestle so that the two of them could settle the matter once and for all. Thus the lines were specifically drawn in this morality play. The wrestling audience saw in the conflict the virtue of self-reliance struggling against the evils of deception and cowardice. In this sense, therefore, the ring war between Tommy Rich and the Superstar took on the nature of a limited scope morality play because there were at war symbols of a specific type of good and a specific type of evil, both consistent with basic morality and values, particularly of the wrestling audience.

While this particular struggle between Tommy Rich and the Superstar epitomizes the approach of professional wrestling to the staging of the conflicts of good and evil, it is but one of many variations on the theme. What does become clear through the example, however, is that the wrestlers' characters and actions conform to the audience's clearly drawn expectations of what good and evil will do. Perhaps an even better example, although one more specifically established within the frame of reference of an American audience, is the conflict between an American patriot figure and an evil foreigner. This discussion will be developed in even greater detail in Chapter Four on character which deals with the archetypal nature of such characters, but our more immediate concern is with the nature of the conflict more than with character to whatever extent the two can be separated.

Although forty years away from the Second World War, Americans, via the reminders of the Korean and Vietnamese conflicts and the Iranian Hostage Crisis, are suspicious of many foreigners who enter the ring. Their purposes cannot be virtuous, for it would be inconsistent with the nature of a foreigner for them to be so. The result of this attitude in professional wrestling is that the most hated of villains are the goose-stepping Nazis and the sneaky Japanese whose ancestors bombed Pearl Harbor. Currently, Arabs are a primary object of hatred for the wrestling audience who cannot forget the bodies of the dead American soldiers that were so flagrantly displayed after the failed attempt to rescue the hostages in Iran. Hussien the Arab, more often known as the Sheik, who throughout the Iranian Crisis boasted his Iranian heritage became perhaps the most hated of villains, particularly after his ring battle with Blackjack Mulligan, a tall, three hundred pound Texan who was quick to point out his "good ol' boy" philosophy and his determination to make Hussien pay for the insults he had bantered about weak Americans. Jack took several beatings from the Arab before finally chasing him from the mid-Atlantic area. More to the point, Jack was constantly taking a beating because he insisted on fighting within the rules even though his adversary was willing to cheat in whatever way was necessary to take the victory. As limited scope morality play material, this conflict presented the stereotypical "good ol' boy," an American folk hero, the cowboy, trying to ward off the infection of the evil and treacherous foreigner. Evil, of course, won several times before being defeated, for in the larger concept of the morality play, evil must be strong if there is to be any dramatic tension. Evil must, however, also be defeated if the drama is to fit into the morality play tradition.

As symbolic as these two feuds are, thus completely in line with the idea of the morality play, the primary focus of this form of medieval drama was to depict the salvation of man's soul. Moreover, the most successful wrestling conflicts in drawing crowd attention are those that dramatize this basic theme. Michael Hayes, the Everyman of professional wrestling, had become a despised figure in the sport because of his constantly interfering in matches between his Freebirds, Terry Gordy and Buddy Roberts, and a series of heroes, including the four hundred pound Stan Frazier and his partner Robert Fuller, a couple of boys who spoke and acted as if they had just come down from the farm. After injuring Stan, Hayes and company had to face Ted Dibiase who joined Fuller in an attempt to avenge Stan's injury. The three heroes were highly popular throughout Georgia because of their honesty and sense of fair play, which more often than not left them defeated and injured at the hands of the Freebirds. Throughout, Hayes was the focus of audience hatred, for it was his constant assertiveness that led the Freebirds to do their worst. However, when the going got tough, Gordy deserted the team, and Hayes had to enter the ring as a wrestler to try and save the Firebirds' championship belts. He was unable to do so and disappeared from the scene while Gordy quickly returned with a new partner who along with him won the belts back. Within a month, Hayes, too, returned rather meekly and told of how his little brother had put him back on the road of decency by accusing him of being a quitter. In a speech reminiscent of John Capaletti's Heisman Trophy acceptance speech, Hayes said that because he saw how true were his brother's words he was going to make it back to the top, this time fighting fairly and beginning by destroying Terry Gordy. Immediately, the audience remembered that Gordy had deserted his friends and that Hayes had entered the ring despite his supposed cowardice. Gordy had violated the moral demands made in wrestling, even of a villain, and Hayes had fought like a hero; therefore, his decision to fight Gordy was exactly the method of redeeming himself in the eyes of the fans. Suddenly, Hayes was joined by a host of hero figures who, despite their having been victims of his past actions, were willing to team up with him. That these men were all willing to forget the past and stand with Hayes clearly indicated that his was more than just a quest for revenge, that his conversion was complete and that he deserved forgiveness now that his intentions were honorable. He was, after all, going after a coward, the worst of villains, guilty of an evil beyond even that of a wrestler who does not obey the rules.

The tremendous popularity Hayes gained in a short time points up that the wrestling audience is more affected by the redemption of a hero than by any other possible outcome to a conflict. The basic clarity of values of the audience allows this quick reversal of attitude as the same quality in a medieval audience allowed the morality play to work. For such audiences, there is no real debate about the perimeters of good and evil; they immediately know which is which. This lack of philosophical complexity made the morality play work five hundred years ago. And while modern philosophy may have confused these distinctions somewhat, the wrestling fan has probably never heard of Kierkegaard or Neitzsche, so he is completely prepared to accept the basic dichotomy of the morality play, even on the stage of the wrestling ring.

Essentially everything that has been said about how professional wrestling employs elements of the morality play is equally accurate in a discussion of professional wrestling as allegory, for the morality play is one of many types of allegory. There is, however, one important point to be made that while applicable to wrestling as a morality play is equally valid in a much broader context. In any allegory, there must be an interest in the characters and actions beyond symbolic function. In other words, the audience must be interested in the characters as persons, not just in their symbolic roles. This requirement is well fulfilled in professional wrestling; every effort is made to keep Tommy Rich, for example, from being just the ideal of American youth. In Rich's case, there is great emphasis by the commentators on Rich's flaws and how these flaws have caused him to fall prey to the Superstar or to lose the World's Championship which he held for only five days. Rich, however, is no exception to this point as the same can be said of many wrestlers, but he serves as an excellent example because he is so unusually popular with the audience.

Tommy Rich is an emotional wrestler whose tendency to lose his temper accounts in large part for his ring behavior. This characteristic, however, is a humanizing element, for as a result he has wrestled as a villain at times when he felt the desire to win while the shackles of wrestling fairly were preventing him from winning matches against lesser opponents. Moreover, Rich is able to wrestle as a villain without completely losing the support of fans who can appreciate his reaction to constantly being defeated by villains whose evil, unlike Rich's, is the product of their rotten core. In fact, the relationship Rich has with the audience is a close one and accounts for his success and shows the extent to which he is treated as an individual, not just as another hero or villain figure. Rich is, in fact, so loved by the fans that a few years ago the wrestling promotion set up a match between Rich and the then World's Champion, Harley Race, by having Rich's mother appear on television with her scrapbook of Tommy's athletic career in baseball, football and, of course, wrestling. So moved by the response of the fans to this ploy, Rich promised to win the championship for them. He did not and, consequently, left Georgia to go home to Nashville "to get his head together." After spending a year or so away and after being announced by a film showing him wandering the Tennessee mountains, Willie Nelson's "On the Road Again" playing in the background, Rich appeared on the scene in Georgia just at the moment that Terry Gordy was about to injure Ted Dibiase, and won the hearts of the fans all over again, announcing that this time he was back to stay.

This rather extended discussion points up that whatever Rich may symbolize about youth and good American ethics, he is also subject to emotions, the kind that individualize us all, thus preventing his being no more than an abstract representation of good. For wrestling to work as theatre as well as allegory, this clear delineation between the man and the symbol is necessary. However much the audience might react to seeing good defeat evil or being defeated by it, their reaction will be greater if the representative of good is one of their own, one who feels the victory or defeat, one who bleeds human not symbolic blood, one who can feel the need to return home and get in touch with himself. Thus, wrestling, whatever it may have in common with allegory and sometimes because of the similarities, is theatre, the basic theatre of life that need not be intellectualized, indeed that resists intellectualization, to be appreciated.

Whatever point that might be made about the relationship between professional wrestling and the various theatrical traditions might well be argued to be incidental rather than calculated. We do not, however, find this to be the case and offer as evidence that the wrestling promotion is well aware of the parallels between the various forms of theatre and the staging of wrestling conflicts, the very clearly designed borrowings from the Noh Drama.

The Japanese Noh Drama dates from the fourteenth century and is one of the most polished and ornamental forms of stagecraft in the history of theatre. It is short and highly symbolic, characterized by harmonious combinations of dance, costume, mime, poetry and music. Of these features, the dance, costume and mime are those most used in the staging of wrestling. To see more clearly the relationship between the Noh Drama and wrestling, let us turn our attention to the wrestler who epitomizes the borrowing in his act, the Great Kabuki.

It is no accident of linguistics that the Great Kabuki has taken as his name a very specific type of Noh Drama, the Kabuki play. The form of the Kabuki play that is paralleled in wrestling is the epic form that represents in the scripts scenes from the heroic age in Japan's history. More specifically, the Kabuki play is designed primarily for spectacle, has an all male cast, and pays close attention to dance. Within the range of the scripts are tales of legendary heroes and feats of daring that typify the Japanese heroic age and that parallel the tales of heroism in western culture found in the epics of Homer and the plays of Aeschylus and Sophocles.

The Great Kabuki typifies a hero from the Kabuki play in every sense. He is a villain on the American wrestling stage only because he is an oriental who is completely oriental in his role playing, not a westernized figure at all. The fact remains, however, that he does epitomize the oriental heroic figure, particularly as set up by the frame of reference of the Noh Drama. He is an accomplished athlete, well skilled in the acrobatics of the martial arts. He adjusts his ring philosophy to that of the snake, the dragon and so on in keeping with oriental tradition, employing different tactics in accord with the specific guise being followed at the moment. Moreover, the

Great Kabuki is ruthless and dangerous in the ring, for an epic hero could not be otherwise, whether in terms of western culture or those of eastern civilization.

Where we can see more specifically the Greak Kabuki's adherence to the Noh Drama tradition, however, is in his use of costume and dance. He enters the ring in elaborate oriental robes, often carrying Samurai swords with which to intimidate his opponent. He wears masks and make-up, supposedly to cover scars on his face left after his face was shoved into burning coals during a match where the purpose was to pin the opponent on top of those same coals. The masks conform to those worn by the actors in a Kabuki play. The one he generally wears is that of a horned demon figure. The Great Kabuki emits green fog from his mouth all through his matches fulfilling in part the demand for spectacle. Finally, he circles symbolically over a fallen opponent in the traditional victor's dance.

What makes the Great Kabuki effective as a villain is the use of these features of the Noh Drama which cause him to appear so very oriental. He, unlike many oriental wrestlers, is not Americanized; thus his mere presence in the ring can stimulate all the negative reactions that Americans have to Japanese as a result of World War II and the Pearl Harbor attack. He has, moreover, during the past been involved in a feud with Dusty Rhodes, the plumber's son who is the epitome of the American hero, above all others who pose in a similar guise. Recently, Dusty appeared in Indian war paint, in a sense a parody of the Great Kabuki, but more a direct challenge to him because it reminded him that Americans too had a historic culture of heroism and bravery that parallels that of the Japanese. Because the Great Kabuki follows the Noh Drama tradition in his role playing, Dusty was allowed to follow effectively a similar one within the American tradition. When this well drawn American folk hero enters the ring against the typical oriental, the classic confrontation of East and West recreates itself week after week in Texas auditoriums and Georgia high school gyms. The near overdose of symbolism is effective, however, because of how specifically the images are drawn from stereotypes of American and Japanese culture.[6]

Other Japanese wrestlers adhere to an extent to the

dictates of Noh Drama. Ninja follows basically the same style of the Great Kabuki in following the Kabuki play tradition. Their approaches work because they have taken and followed closely an unfamiliar form of theatre that Americans recognize only at a surface level. The American audience does not see theatre at work directly and can, therefore, accept the reality suggested more easily. Their direct borrowings, however, clearly establish that the wrestling promoters know exactly what they are doing when they use theatrical traditions in setting the roles and conflicts the wrestler will play out.

While we have thus far examined the way professional wrestling parallels the morality play, allegory and Noh Drama in establishing its thematic design and its staging, it is the parallel between wrestling and the Greek and Roman theatre that provides the basic techniques of staging of the sport. The parallel is substantial and in large part explained because of the similarity of problems of a vast audience and large distances between audience and stage that professional wrestling and Greek and Roman drama share. Peter Arnott, a well known scholar of classical drama, explains, "the open air theatre dictates its own terms; acting must necessarily be broader than indoors; and this was particularly true in Greek theatre with its vast audience."[7] Precisely the same point could well be made about the problems faced by the performers in a wrestling match that occurs in a large coliseum, in an outdoor arena, or on television where the distance between performer and audience is one of the medium. Arnott characterizes the accommodations that the actor was forced to make as a "system of movements unambiguous in meaning and perceptible even to the spectators furthest from the stage."[8] Again, what Arnott says about the classical theatre explains the theatrics of the professional wrestler whose gestures and wrestling holds symbolize for the audience not close enough to the ring to observe facial expressions or hear comments exactly what feelings of pain, fear or frustration the wrestler is supposedly feeling. Paul Gallico discusses these movements and the communication they effect between wrestler and audience as being related in some ways to mime. "Never mind that the villain, himself an accomplished mummer, is holding Tsimmie's tootsies in a manner that would not injure a two-year-old child. We in the audience educated in the symbols of classical tragedy, know that this is the Dreaded Toe Hold calculated to send spasms of fearful and well nigh unbearable pain through the victim."[9] Gallico's somewhat tongue-in-cheek comment makes several significant points. The most important of these is that the audience must be educated in the wrestler's art; they must be able to recognize the holds and what they mean in terms of generating pain or possibly causing the opponent to submit. They do not, then, need a verbal expression to know that their hero is in danger or that the villain is getting what he deserves. The persons in the upper decks, moreover, are as aware of the pain the hold causes as are those at ringside who might hear a moan or some other verbal expression. Expressing meaning through exaggerated movement was exactly the technique used by the Greek and Roman actors to express intense emotion. Oedipus, realizing that his fate has defeated him, would have thrown up his left hand, a symbol of grief and unendurable pain more intense than his words could reflect or his face could show from behind a mask. A wrestler held to the mat and tortured would in similar fashion kick his legs like a kid throwing a tantrum to let the audience know that he is in fact hurt even if the menacing arm bar looks less than torturous.

More than just their holds, however, wrestlers use other stock movements to communicate with the audience. A wrestler giving in to the referee's commands will raise both hands above his head to indicate compliance. Regularly, wrestlers will fall on both knees in a corner and shake their heads to indicate they want a pause in their opponents' attacks. We in the audience know, however, from experience that this is in reality a villain's ploy to take his opponent off guard; a hero would never ask for mercy. This is the point, moreover, that needs to be stressed. The movements by the actors in Greek and Roman theatre were used to communicate with an audience that knew the story and knew what was going to happen, movements or not; they were simply part of the actor's art. So it is in professional wrestling. The audience knows the basic plot; they have seen it often enough. They know as well the meaning of the movements. Only a novice would not realize that when one wrestler wraps his arms around the head of his opponent he is applying the sleeper hold which will render in only a matter of seconds even the biggest brute unconscious. But when he wraps his arms slightly differently, he is only using a chin lock that does nothing but allow him to control his opponent's movement. Yet, while in both classical theatre and professional wrestling many of the movements may be unnecessary, they are part of the actor's responsibility in communicating effectively with both the ringside ticket holder and the viewer with the balcony seat.

A second point that can be well made about the parallels between professional wrestling and classical theatre is that both use costumes to achieve the same effect, to identify the roles of the characters. Again, let us set the framework for this discussion by noting Professor Arnott's observations about costuming in classical theatre. "The effect of the ... formal costume was to depersonalize the tragic actor, in the same way that the neutral setting gave a timeless quality to the drama."[10] This depersonalization through costume resulted from the fact that the same basic costumes were worn by all kings, all prostitutes, all slaves, and so on. As a result, the audience immediately knew the role of the actor and what to expect from him. While in professional wrestling the distinctions are not nearly so clear cut with there being a significantly larger cast of character types, specific costumes do signal specific types of characters. What we are less likely to be able to distinguish by costume alone is which characters are villains and which are heroes, mainly because most wrestlers vacillate between the two without changing any other aspects of their characters. What costumes generally accomplish is to identify each wrestler's concept of himself. If he is a "good ol' boy," he will wear cowboy boots and a western hat, perhaps even a vest for a warmup jacket. We will see this and know in large part what we can expect from him in the ring. We will, moreover, know whom he will not like. A "good ol' boy" never likes foreigners for example. He is a wrestler who will fight tough, not accept help, admit it if he cheats; he is a wrestler who makes no pretensions. His ethic will be one of survival of the fittest, not necessarily the smartest; if anything he takes pride in his ignorance and simplicity for they are characteristics of one who came up the hard way, without the benefits of education or money, but made it to the top by working hard and beating the daylights out of anyone who got in the way. As a result, he may not be smart, but neither is he scared.

A wrestler who wears lavish robes, on the other hand, is more likely to survive in the ring because of his cunning. He will boast of his money, cars and women. He will do anything to win and prevent having a scar left on his face of self-proclaimed beauty. His costly robe is a symbol both to himself and to the audience of his success, obtained by whatever means are necessary. He, also unlike the "good ol' boy," will lie about cheating and say that he is simply smarter than his victim who did not have the brain power to find some way of winning. About three years ago, Mid Atlantic wrestling featured a confrontation between two such wrestlers, the "good ol' boy" Blackjack Mulligan and "Nature Boy" Rick Flair. What was interesting, however, was that rather than attack each other they went after each other's costume. Flair destroyed Mulligan's cowboy hat, supposedly given to him by Waylon Jennings, while Jack responded by ripping apart Flair's ten thousand dollar robe. Their actions represented well the contempt they had for each other's way of life, thus the costume's symbolic functions increased to the point of making their feud much more than it would have been were they simply two wrestlers trying to win a match. More could be said here about costumes and their roles as symbols, but further discussion will be presented in the chapter on character.

One final point that Arnott makes about costuming in classical theatre that well applies to the current discussion about wrestling is about how costumes restricted characters and the actors' methods of handling them. "He was at liberty to improvise and, to an extent, to color the role by his own personality, but only within the limits that the mask and costume imposed on him."[11] Applied to wrestling, Arnott's comment points up the fact that a wrestler is somewhat confined by his role which must be consistent with the costume he wears. Whether hero or villain, he must conform to the behavior patterns of the "good ol' boy," the punk rocker or whatever image he has assumed. Austin Idol, for example, who has been both hero and villain, cannot suddenly start acting like a brawling truck driver. He cannot, moreover, simply take off his bright red, full length trunks and put on a John Deere hat to effect this change. He has identified himself with one image, and the audience would be disturbed by a change. He can become either villain or good guy if he chooses without changing costumes, however, simply by choosing a more evil villain or more virtuous hero as an opponent. It is at this level that we can see the individuality Arnott allows taking over within the confines of role and costume identification. Perhaps the best case in point would be the situation faced by Bob Roop, the 1968 U.S. Olympic heavyweight wrestler. Roop wore his Olympic trunks and decorated them with symbols of the American flag when he became a professional wrestler. From then on he was the American kid next door, even when he wrestled as a villain and became the kid gone bad.

This final point takes us back to the section on the influence of the morality play and allegory. The association of costumes and roles suggests the universal nature of wrestling which makes the sport a kind of twentieth-century morality play. Yet, allegory demands that there be more than a universal statement and that the audience have interest in the characters as individuals. This demand, too, is well allowed by the options that each wrestling character has, even if within prescribed limits. We can, therefore, see within the conflicts that emerge between hero and villain something that touches our lives on a basic, not just universal, level. When Bob Armstrong, former fireman, and Mr. Saito, Japanese sneak, wrestle we see both the clash of east and west as well as the struggle of Bob, the "good ol' boy," and Saito, the evil foreigner. Both conflicts, moreover, can be recognized the moment the wrestlers enter the ring, Bob in simple Olympic tights and Saito in an oriental robe.

Having taken up the issue of professional wrestling as theatre, we feel compelled to conclude with Aristotle for what may be obvious reasons. First, ever since Aristotle made his basic pronouncement on the nature of drama, particularly tragedy, essentially every critical theory applied to the art of the stage has either reiterated, reinterpreted or redefined basic Aristotelian principles, this or it has reacted against the dictums of the Greek philosopher. In either case, Aristotle is the point of departure. Second, wrestling saw its beginnings in Western culture in the Hellenic world, more particularly in the Greek Olympics. More important, however, although certainly more subjective, whenever we sit in the Omni in Atlanta or the Charlotte Coliseum and witness the conflicts of such titanic figures as Blackjack Mulligan, Bruiser Brody or Stan Hanson, we feel time has reversed its movement, that we have somehow joined Priam on the walls of Troy and are witnessing the tragic duel between Acheleus and Hektor. Such extraordinary figures, or at least the legends of such figures, gave rise to the whole Hellenic culture and in turn to the society that produced Aristotle and the drama on which Aristotle based his dramatic theory.

Quite simply, Aristotle defined tragedy, the dramatic genre generally closest in nature to professional wrestling, as the representation of a serious and complete action of great magnitude, presented on the stage, as opposed to being narrated, and arousing the emotions of pity and fear in the audience in order to achieve a purgation of those emotions. The basic elements of tragedy in the order that Aristotle emphasizes their importance are action, character, thought, diction, music and spectacle.[13] Professional wrestling not only conforms to the general definition, but also employs all the component parts of the genre. The end product tends to be distinctly Aristotelian although professional wrestling does emphasize the elements in a different order, giving particular stress to character and spectacle.

Certainly professional wrestling is the representation of an action. In fact most of its detractors complain that it is just that rather than an action itself. The point needs no debate. The action is also complete as it is dictated as ending with a pin fall, submission or disqualification. The conflict of characters may continue as through a Greek trilogy, but there are individual and complete actions along the way. Even the continuing conflicts will finally end in a cage match or some other decisive conflict between characters. The seriousness, indeed the magnitude, is determined by the allegorical nature of the conflicts. Rarely do we see simply two men at war. The promotion works too diligently to instill a sense of values into the ring wars, values that qualify the conflict of good and evil although this is the basis of all conflict in professional wrestling and thus accounts for the magnitude of the ring wars.

One need only attend one wrestling event to see the extent to which the audiences' emotions are aroused. They, in what we consider the epitome of suspended disbelief, are people who want their emotions ignited; thus they willingly accept the hype that is inherent in the dramas to achieve this end. So effective is the drama and so entranced is the audience that often members of the crowd will leap into the ring or attack a villain as he leaves his dressing room. Yes, their emotions are evoked, generally, however, in a positive fashion. Psychologists tend to feel that the emotional release is a healthy one, for people can vent frustrations from their jobs and homes and then return purged of hostility. They do so despite the outcome of the matches, for it was after all not real.

Now, let us look closely at the ingredients, the formative elements, of tragedy as defined by Aristotle.

Action, we have dealt with in some detail already. What is worth noting here, however, is that the primary action of the drama of professional wrestling is not that which takes place in the ring. Rather, in the matches at the civic center and gym, we see the denouement of a plot that was established through the television medium. From the characters' challenges and debates that have occurred on television we have become familiar with that which motivates the action; the conflict in the ring is purely the actualization of the already established complication. More to the point, the final conflict in the ring is the fifth act of the drama that has reached its climactic point before we even arrive at the matches. We have seen the threats, the spontaneous attacks, the villainy, the rescues. At the matches we see the resolution, the pistols drawn at daybreak if you will.

Just as Shakespeare found the essence of drama to be character, so too does professional wrestling despite Aristotle's conviction. Actually, character is so important that the next chapter of the book will be devoted to explication of this important point. Aristotle felt that characters in tragedy must be men of great stature. Such stature in professional wrestling is easily established by the physical dimension of the wrestlers. Andre the Giant, of course, is the ideal example as he stands seven feet, four inches and weighs a proportioned 500 pounds. Moreover, most wrestlers, despite some lack of awareness of the critics of the sport, are physical specimens. They have generally established their physical prowess before even entering the professional wrestling ring. Bob Roop and Ken Patera were Olympians. Jack and Jerry Brisco were collegiate champions. Paul Orndorf, Wahoo McDaniels and Ernie Ladd were professional football players, as were Otis Sistrunk and Bobby Hart. Mike Jackson and the Superstar, on the other hand, boast graduate degrees. The real stature of the characters, of course, comes from their allegorical function. Tommy Rich, the epitome of good, has over the years arrived on the scene just in time to rescue a fallen good guy and beat back the onslaught of a villainous character about to do his worst. Tommy may be small of stature, but he is a titanic figure of good who generally defeats evil.

Thought, too, follows from the allegorical structure of professional wrestling. Yet, here perhaps we must say goodbye to Aristotle. The basic ethic is actually quite simple. Professional wrestling is, after all, drama for the masses. For them, good and evil are clear, and good must eventually defeat evil. There is no great complexity of thought as a result. We have in professional wrestling no Hamlet or Oedipus debating the nature of choice in a universe that seems to hold no right action. Diction, too, for it follows from thought, is likewise simple. Yet, in the integral simplicity of the two we do see a quality of great art, that or organicism. Thought is simple, therefore, diction must follow or else the audience would be taken unaware. That the two follow together is perfect harmony for in doing so character and action are kept at the proper level for the audience.

When we discuss music in Greek drama, we are basically dealing with the function of the chorus, both including music in the sense of sound and words as well as in the sense of simply words spoken in rhythm. Professional wrestling occasionally employs music in the first sense; the Freebirds' entrance is announced by the song of that name. But the idea of words spoken in verse does not exist. The real parallel is that between the function of the Greek chorus and the function of the wrestling commentator. This function is crucial to the staging to the wrestling drama. In Greek drama, the chorus was the vehicle through which the audience experienced the drama. The chorus gave the audience the knowledge they needed to fully comprehend the nature of the conflicts in the specific play. Also, the chorus gave insight into how the audience should react to certain situations. In essence the audience experienced the drama vicariously through the chorus. The wrestling commentator does just this for the professional wresting fan.

Certainly the most successful wrestling commentator is Gordon Solie who broadcasts in Georgia and in Florida. The shows he handles are internationally syndicated. Solie gives the audience the immediate information they need about holds, about the prowess of the combatants, and so on. But his function goes far beyond this alone. He tells us all we need to know to comprehend the drama taking place and to react to it. He tells us the reputations of the wrestlers and why they are combatting each other with such ferocity. He tells us about their families and their lives so that they become fully developed characters for us, not mere representations in the ring of some allegorical virtues or vices. When necessary to explain the conflict he shows films of recent matches so that our frame of reference is complete for us to understand the nature of a specific conflict. This historical scene setting is precisely what the Greek chorus did in the prologue to a Greek drama when they set the stage of the play by telling the legendary material that led a specific character, Oedipus for example, to his moment of crisis, his finding the murderer of Laius.

Solie, again like the Greek chorus in a Greek play, does more however. He also signals the moral response we in the audience should have to a given situation. Recently, commenting on the rift that took place between Roddy Piper and his onetime friend Playboy Gary Hart, Solie introduced Hart as follows: "In Christian history it was Judas, to the Romans, Brutus, and in America it was Benedict Arnold...." Clearly, Solie was making a powerful moral assessment of the man he was introducing by comparing him with a long line of traitors. Solie, therefore, provided the frame of reference for the audience to use as they viewed the upcoming conflict between the converted Piper and Hart's man the Great Kabuki. The idea of wrestling commentator as chorus, or sports commentator in general, is a fascinating one; however, one that we leave to another scholar to develop more completely.

Finally, spectacle is the last of Aristotle's formative elements. It is, nonetheless, the essence of professional wrestling. It encompasses the finery of costume, the grandeur of staging, and all the trappings that make professional wrestling a drama in the highest sense, but sport in perhaps the lowest. We say this, however, remembering Terry Funk's comment to an interviewer that she would think less of him if he walked into the ring followed by a group of skimpily clad women who set off a cannon everytime he scored a pinfall. Of course, he was parodying the idea of professional football in his remarks and pointing up that other sports do engage in their own forms of spectacle. However, professional wrestling pivots on this element.

One must quickly notice after all this that the elements which professional wrestling emphasizes and Aristotle did not are precisely those elements, spectacle over diction and thought for example, that make the drama of the wrestlers a drama for the popular, not the intellectual audience.

Were P.T. Barnum alive today and still trying to incorporate professional wrestling into his acts with the circus, he would probably find the modern form of the sport even more effective than the semi-legitimate competition he presented in his own day. The old style matches did not have near the elements of spectacle the sport now has and held little appeal for the spectators who came to see freaks, clowns, circus animals and daring feats, something more akin to contemporary professional wrestling. Today's elaborate drama, therefore, would fit well into this arena of side show thrill. Indeed, much of the attraction of modern professional wrestling is its kinship with the county fair midway. The audience, too, comes from the same segment of the population that will pay a quarter to see the bearded lady. They are spectators who are wise enough to understand the symbols and conflicts without being so wise as to worry about the hype. Not that they are a simple-minded bunch. Quite the contrary, the wrestling audience, like the man we discussed at the beginning of this chapter, know what they have put their five bucks down to see, and when they do not get it they can become an angry lot. They will send catcalls at the first sign that the performers are about to break the illusion. Therefore, the audience has itself demanded that the wrestling promotion search all corners of theatrical fare to find the correct combination of approaches to present theme and staging in such a way that will please a demanding group. After all, a wrestling fan may realize that what he is watching is hype, but he wants it to be good hype. The nature of the audience also demands that stock theatrical conventions be used. These work best because the wrestling fan does not want to have to think too much; if he did he would be at a performance of *Hamlet*. That is not why he is at the matches. He wants to know evil when he sees it; he wants to know what the moves mean; he is a passive audience intellectually, but his emotions are on fire. Thus he can and will respond to the exaggerated themes and stagecraft as long as he does not have to dwell on what they mean. Therefore, the basic morality play structure and the costumes and gestures of the classical theatre work well. He understands these and reponds to them. We are, therefore, quite accurate in classifying professional wrestling as one of the popular arts, for it is one designed for a general audience, one not overly sophisticated; the same audience that enjoys other simple forms of theatre— the soap opera, country music, a good car race with plenty of crashes—the audience that does in fact shape our basic social and cultural ethic and aesthetic.

Notes

[1]This rehearsal is not to be equated with the practice of an athlete, for it includes both opponents working together to choreograph their moves rather than improving their skills used to defeat each other.

[2]Edward Francisco wrote for the University of Tennessee *Daily Beacon* and dealt with the night's events in his weekly column.

[3]T. Hendricks, "Professional Wrestling as Moral Order," *Sociological Inquiry*, 44:3 (1974), 178.

[4]Leo Rothsten, "America Hails a New Art Form," *Look*, 17 (February 24, 1953), 89.

[5]C. Hugh Holman, *A Handbook to Literature*, 3rd ed. (Indianapolis:

Odyssey Press, 1978), p. 328.

[6]For a complete discussion of the nature of stereotypes and particularly the importance of understanding stereotypes in the popular arts, see Deming and Wahlstrom, "Chasing the Popular Arts Through the Critical Forest," *Journal of Popular Culture*, 13:3 (Winter 1980).

[7]Peter D. Arnott, *The Ancient Greek and Roman Theatre* (New York: Random House, 1971), pp. 44-45.

[8]*Ibid.*, p. 43.

[9]Paul Gallico, "That Was Acting," *Theatre Arts*, 33, January 1949, 27.

[10]Arnott, p. 44.

[11]*Ibid.*, p. 51.

Chapter Four
The Participants

It was now that Grendel, the enemy of God who had wantonly committed numberless atrocities against the human race, discovered that his bodily strength was of no use when the valiant kinsman of Hygelac had got hold of him by the claw. Neither would give the other quarter. The fiend suffered excruciating pain. An enormous wound became visible in his shoulder; his sinews snapped, and tendons burst. Victory was Beowulf's.

Beowulf

The Wrestling Villains

In the fall of 1981 Rick Flair, who had recently defeated Dusty Rhodes for the NWA World's Heavyweight Wrestling Championship belt, entered the Greensboro Coliseum to defend his title against Ricky Steamboat. For ten years Flair had toured the Carolinas, sometimes as a villain but more recently as a genuine hero for throngs of adamant wrestling fans in one of the real hotbeds for the sport. Since winning the belt he had been on a world tour, defending his title. Word had reached his fans that Flair had changed, that his new found glory had gone to his head. He was, they heard, fighting the way he had in the past, doing anything to win a match and keep the crown, the fame, the glory, the money that came with being the champion. Ricky Steamboat, on the other hand, remained a local favorite as he entered this match with his old friend, the man with whom he'd campaigned to rid the Mid Atlantic region of various villains.

That, however, was all past. Their match was brutal and quickly took on the flavor of most top bills, each wrestler combining an equal amount of wrestling and brawling tactics. At the end, Flair was victorious, though badly beaten. Steamboat lay dazed in the middle of the ring. Flair started toward the dressing room amid a mixture of cheers and catcalls from both former and still fans. As he did, Sergeant Slaughter and his privates, Jim Nelson and the former good guy Don Kernodal, attacked the ring to do further damage to Steamboat with whom they had been feuding during recent months. Unable to fight back against three men, Steamboat took a severe beating until, to everyone's surprise, Flair stopped and returned to the ring, no doubt to add to the massacre. However, instead he attacked Slaughter and company. Together he and Steamboat were able to fight off the assault by the Marines, but not until Flair had been knocked unconscious when Slaughter used the champ's belt as a weapon against him. Steamboat, himself bleeding from several lacerations, lifted Flair to his shoulders and carried him from the ring, the man whom he had earlier been trying with all his skill to defeat, but also the man who had, no doubt because of some remaining feelings about their past friendship, just risked his own safety to rescue him.

Perhaps narrating this event should color what one would try to say about the wrestling villain, but it does demonstrate the most crucial point to this discussion, that the wrestling villain can become a hero on the scale of Sidney Carton in Dicken's *Tale of Two Cities* very quickly if the right circumstances exist for the audience to buy the conversion. In this case, the circumstances were right. Flair was in front of home folks who knew him as a hero. He was, moreover, acting out of what appeared to be deep felt feelings of friendship for another real hero figure. He was, and this is crucial, rescuing this hero from the assault of a Marine drill sergeant, a person to be feared in American culture for every man who ever went through boot camp or anyone else who has ever seen a war movie. In other words, Slaughter was the perfect foil for a moral conversion, for he had established himself as a genuine villain.

Slaughter does, nonetheless, have an army of renegade wrestling fans who dress in military garb and who address him with salutes when he enters the ring. Obvious, therefore, in this discussion is the need to qualify any generalizations that are made about the wrestling villain. Generalizations will be helpful of course, but always they must be regarded as just that and qualified to whatever extent will be possible.

As a general definition the wrestling villain is a man or woman who breaks the rules in the ring in an effort to win a match. He/she pulls hair, hits an opponent who is on the ropes, pulls the opponent's trunks to escape a hold, gouges eyes, uses foreign objects pulled from the trunks, etc. The simplicity of this definition, however, almost renders it useless. More appropriate, the wrestling villain in some way violates the sense of justice that the audience follows by representing either literally or symbolically evil that preys upon good. The villain may be a staunch Russian communist or a cowboy in a black hat. He may be a manager who interferes in matches or a punk rocker. One thing is certain; without him there would be no professional wrestling, for if there is one thing the fans hate it is a wrestling match between two good guys.

By design professional wrestling depicts the conflict of good and evil. Good fighting good is simply too boring; it is like a car race without a crash. Also, evil is too interesting to do without. A simple reminder of Milton's Satan in *Paradise Lost* and the grandness of his character points up how interesting evil is. Whatever interest good has in professional wrestling follows from the fact that good may someday defeat evil, or better, good may be converted by evil.

A final point needs to be made before we look at the individual types of villains, that point being that the success of professional wrestling is determined by the fact that the fans who attend the matches are able to release their hostilities. They see in the villains the foreman who gave them a bad day, the rude telephone worker, the customer who wrote the false check. All the feelings of anger that they have kept stored inside out of a sense of social decorum can flood forth. The beating the villain takes can become for the fans the beating that someone else deserved. Most psychologists who have looked at this phenomenon agree that the release is a healthy one. They see the catharsis the fans experience as similar to that they would experience at a play. This is, however, not high tragedy. This is low drama, drama for the masses, and the masses want to see villains they can recognize and therefore more easily hate.

If hate were all there were to it, then perhaps those who worry about the values that wrestling projects might have a legitimate concern. However, what the example at the beginning of this chapter suggests is that the real drama of the wrestling script occurs when a villain changes his spots and becomes a hero, even if for only one match. The capacity to change, and for the audience to accept the change, is the ultimate characteristic of the villain and this capacity to change is in large part, because the audience will accept it, the secret to seeing the decent morality in the wrestling script.

When one begins to discuss the wrestling villain and to identify the various types, the ability of the villain to change is an essential concern. It is in fact the vascillating nature of the wrestling villains that colors their archetypal or stereotypical nature, although even these changes are within the context of the conflict of good and evil. Bob Roop, former Olympic heavyweight division wrestler and now wrestling villain, explains the necessity of the wrestlers' changing from black hat to white and back again as being an appeal to the audience's desire for an almost religious conversion in the villains. As Roop puts it, when the villain splits from his companions and seeks out a local hero to help him avenge some vile wrong suffered at the hands of his former compatriots, the people stream to the arenas to see "Satan and Jesus Christ as tag team partners."[1] This is an interesting phenomenon, often paralleled by the fall from grace of a hero as a stock ploy used to ignite audience interest in the ring wars. For again the audience will turn out to see their former idol receive the beating he deserves for his moral corruption and possibly return to his former virtue. In this sense, the hero, although certainly more often the villain, fits well into the scapegoat tradition, for in both cases the audience sees such a character punished for his fall as a sacrificial victim who, by taking a beating, of which they approve, purges them of their own moral backsliding. In an appeal to the critical work of Northrop Frye, Wahlstrom and Deming give an excellent analysis of this type of situation: "Each culture engages in a continuous internal dialectic that traces the dimensions of the culture's desires and fears. When the dialectic is articulated visually, it becomes icon. When it is acted out it becomes ritual, a ceremony of some sort with an established form or method of performance."[2] The ritual of wrestling, then, is the moral dilemma of the wrestlers manifested by their constantly changing roles. The heroes represent society's desires, the villains, its evil. The next section will deal with the heroes; our concern here is identifying those many villain types that fill the *dramatis personae* of the wrestling drama and discussing what the existence of each tells about the mores of the wrestling fans.

The most distinctive of the villains is the evil foreigner, the Machivellian of Renaissance literature, who especially in this time of world tension represents a justification of American distrust of foreigners. Throughout the cold war, the Vietnam period, and the Iranian Hostage Crisis, this character has been an especially effective scapegoat for the American audience. Because he is wicked, we can legitimately hate him and relish in the beating he takes from an American hero. The release of this hostility by the fans well relieves the frustrations Americans have felt because of trying international situations. There is no need for guilt, for the villain deserves the hatred he receives. The better the beating he receives, the better the audience will feel. In recent years and in response to very tense international situations in the Middle East particularly there has been a significant rise in the number of flag waving heroes who decidedly make their ring wars with evil foreigners represent the surge of patriotism that Americans feel in times of crisis.

The appearance of the evil foreigner is not, however, dependent on an immediate international crisis; he is a constant in the wrestling script. Any fan who lost a loved one at Pearl Harbor, in Vietnam or Korea, who fought in World War II, can appreciate seeing a German Nazi, a Japanese Sneak, or a Russian Communist get the beating he deserves if not for his own sins then for those of his fathers. Such nationalities are clearly those who most often appear in the wrestling ring; however, Lord Alfred Hayes, the English nobleman with the splendid speech, can enlist hatred as did his fathers who closed Boston Harbor. For this reason, one can clearly see that the stereotypical element exists. Every culture has its particular villains from its particular history. The wrestling script, therefore, is not limited to enacting contemporary conflicts; it can dig deep into American heritage and find numerous suitable objects for our hatred.

One of the most successful evil foreigners is the Russian

Boris Malenko. For over twenty years he has terrorized wrestling fans with his savagery and his Russian nationalism. Unlike most wrestling villains, Malenko has never wrestled as a hero so thoroughly is he associated with evil by the wrestling fans. Perhaps the most effective script Malenko ever played was one that dominated Tennessee wrestling for months during 1979. Wrestling out of Knoxville, Malenko decided that he was best suited to managing the careers of other wrestlers; therefore, he bought the contract of Jerry Blackwell, a four hundred pound Georgia farmboy.

Although he had been a villain in the past, Blackwell appeared to the Tennessee fans as a reserved and kind man who only used his awesome strength to destroy his opponents because Malenko kept appearing on television warning him that if he did not he and his family would lose their farm which for whatever reason was tied up in their contractual agreement. Assuming the Simon Legree image, Malenko became so hated that he was even attacked by specatators on occasion. Finally, just when it appeared the farm was lost, the local hero Ronnie Garvin rushed in, paid the mortgage on the land, and released Blackwell to take his revenge on Malenko. He did so viciously, much to the delight of the fans. All the pieces fit for genuine drama; Malenko assumed the posture of slaveholder, wicked banker, manager, all this on top of his being a Russian tyrant abusing good ol' American boys. Blackwell's revenge was revenge for the audience who had at this point grown to identify with him and his suffering.

In similar fashion, the Arab The Great Mephisto seems an obvious agent of Satan, not just because of the abbreviated form of Mephistopholes of his name, but also because of his ability to corrupt American wrestling Fausts with his promises of fame and fortune. For a long period of time, longer than the usual drama, he managed Maniac Mark Lewin whose wild and vicious ring antics made him appear to be genuinely possessed. Lewin left in his wake a long trail of mangled bodies, most of whom he had finished with his deadly sleeper hold that supposedly left some wrestlers permanently asleep. When Lewin had problems with a wrestler, he simply hurled him from the ring where Mephisto, in appropriate demonic fashion, burned the man. The final assault on American integrity came from Mephisto's ability to prevent his man's suspension through manipulating the courts. His utilization of the free justice system to keep his man in the ring hurting other wrestlers was the final insult. A long line of wrestlers formed to take a shot at Mephisto and Lewin, including some notorious villains who saw the evil of their ways or who at least saw Mephisto as going beyond a villainy they could accept. Finally, it was another of Mephisto's men, Abdullah the Butcher, who accomplished the defeat of Lewin when Mephisto lost control of his camp. The moral, of course, is that evil will finally feed upon itself and in the end be its own destruction; Mephisto had not been able to control that which he had started and was destroyed by his own corruption. This basic theme is integral to the psychomachia drama and the morality play already discussed.

A second wrestling villain is the outlaw figure, generally from Texas, who brandishes cowboy boots and hat, uses such devastating holds as the bulldog and the lariat and fights in such conflicts as the Texas Death Match and the bunkhouse match, altogether presenting the hired gun image of the western killers in the cowboy movies. Even the names of these wrestlers sound ominious and evil: Blackjack Mulligan, Stan "the Man" Hanson, The Hangman, Jake "the Snake" Roberts. Yet, they are the stuff of which heroes can be made, especially folk heroes so popular with the lower-class audience of professional wrestling. The ethic of these villains who come across as real men is clear. They are as willing to take a beating as give one. They believe in settling feuds in the middle of the ring, for that is their job. They seldom fall back on treachery; they are simply vicious. So in essence, theirs is a moral stance, very much in line with what could be called the American ethic of fair play.

The problem with these men is that they are quick tempered and generally willing to fight anyone, including a genuine good guy, for the right money. They are in fact hired guns. They do not have to have a personal grudge against a man to go out and destroy him. If the money is there, they will do it. In this sense, these villains are much like the bounty hunter of the American western movie, more particularly like the renegade lawman who finally decides that he can no longer fight for the wrong side, for the wrestling outlaw villain is, more than any other type of bad guy, capable of quickly becoming a good guy.

An outlaw's acceptance as a hero generally comes when he starts a feud with some other villain, particularly an evil foreigner type. Because the outlaw villain, however bad he might be, is drawn from American folk lore, he can easily convert and be accepted by the audience when he stands up to represent American ethics. A case in point is the feud that took place several years ago and that dominated Georgia wrestling for several weeks. The feud was between Stan "the Man" Hanson and Abdullah the Butcher. Abdullah presented the image of the geek as the carny of wrestling would call it. He would appear on television eating raw chicken and abusing everyone, including the commentator, and generally running roughshod over all the "good ol' boys" from Georgia who entered the ring against him. What was worse, he would attack referees and then after matches were over continue to abuse his fallen victims. These actions made him a perfect target for the equally vicious Hanson who claimed that once the match was over he was unwilling to hurt his opponents further, no matter how much he had hurt them during the conflict. In a sense, Hanson had taken the ethical stand that what happened during the match was part of the business, a fairly common approach even by the hero of wrestling. By taking after Abdullah and rushing into the ring to protect fallen wrestlers, Hanson quickly cleaned up his image. During the feud, Hanson was joined by a host of other heroes who welcomed him to their ranks, even though he had injured many of them in the past, thus initiating the "Jesus and Satan as tag team partners" syndrome. In terms of the drama, Stan's actions represented the moral conversion that suggests a clearly defined hierarchy of values which puts above all else the love of country and the ideals of fair play, both of which are ideals far outweighing the past villainy of a wrestler like Hanson. Because this image of the hired gun who could quickly represent right worked so effectively, it is one Hanson has kept. He vascillates often between the roles of villain and hero, but always within these predictable perimeters; thus the audience is always willing to accept the changes he makes.

A third villain, perhaps less traditional and more the product of contemporary society, is the narcissistic brawler, proud of his own beauty and talents while condescending towards his foes. Such villains earn the disgust of the audience by their pompous, boasting arrogance and especially by speaking with contempt not only of their foes but also the members of the audience themselves. The original of this type of villain and no doubt the most famous wrestler of all time was Gorgeous George (Wagner), whose flashy tights and immaculately kept hair set a standard that has been followed by numerous wrestlers and by his most famous disciple, Muhammad Ali. The current NWA Champion, Rick Flair, is very consciously taking his character from the type George made popular. Perhaps what makes this type of villain so detested is that he is much out of place in the wrestling ring. He is a complete contradiction to the rugged he-man qualities a wrestler "should" have. In other words, he doesn't fit; he breaks the norm; he destroys the order, yet he survives the ring wars. Currently Austin Idol and Flair are the best examples of this archetypal villain. Both are built like power lifters and sport long, bleached blonde hair, giving them the physical appeal of a Mr. Universe. In addition to their wrestling prowess, they boast a harem of women who accompany them on their Lear Jet flights between cities, a showcase of fine cars and beautiful houses and Florida condominiums. In other words, they have acquired the American dream, only to soil it with their pompous boasting about their accomplishments. Therefore, just as they tarnish the whole image of the wrestling business by not appearing as the typical athlete, so too do they affront the American image as completely as do the foreign villains.

A specific example will illustrate how well the narcissistic villain works into the scheme of the wrestling drama. In a recent series of World Championship matches, Rick Flair had to meet the massive negro wrestler "Bad, Bad" Leroy Brown. Brown claims to have grown up in south Chicago where he learned his street brawling tactics. He wrestles in ragged overalls and construction worker's boots. Brown, therefore, contrasts effectively with Flair who wears elaborate rhine stone robes and brags about his fortune and jet set lifestyle.

Through several arm wrestling matches Brown was able to wrestle Flair to a draw. Finally Brown defeated Flair. The next week, however, they appeared again with Flair offering Brown a present to apologize for the previous brawl. However, he also demanded one more arm wrestling match. Brown again won, and Flair again attacked him with the help of another wrestler. He then pulled from the package a bright red cabby's hat and pulled it down over the shaken Brown's eyes.

What this extended example illustrates, besides the definite racial connotations that wrestling never touched twenty years ago, is the conflict of life styles. Flair is the rich and successful villain who is too proud of his ability to accept the abilities of others, especially those who in any way surpass him. Brown, as the poor boy who made good, is exactly the antithesis of Flair. Theirs is a traditional conflict in art. Dicken's *Tale of Two Cities* comes quickly to mind, although many other examples are obvious. The Dickens reference, however, well anticipates the end of the story of Leroy Brown, for like the French revolutionaries who became obsessed with their power, Brown turned to a manager who could help him achieve the fame and fortune of a Flair. In doing so, he set forth on a path of evil and rule breaking akin to that of the man who had humiliated him. The constant temptations of money and a high lifestyle were too great, especially after his conflict with Flair indicated that good does not always prevail.

In a sense, the drama of Leroy Brown illustrates the appeal that the narcissistic villains have with the audience. They tend to have a cult of fans who are attracted to them as Eve was attracted to the forbidden fruit. This is especially true of the young who are thrilled by the bright lights of the jet-set life style that such a villain lives. To intensify the response of those who want it and those who distrust it, Rick Flair appears often stepping onto a Lear Jet with an entourage of female admirers in tow. To the extent that the young thus see him as an idol figure, the older generation who understand the transitory nature of these values see Flair as a villain, for he is corrupting the young. Clearly, therefore, we see the generation gap take form as villainy is determined by the different responses of youth and age. Much the same can be said of the punk rocker villain who is in essence an extension of the narcissistic villain but one even more attuned to contemporary society.

Much of the discussion in this book has focused on the
Fabulous Freebirds whose lives, in the ring and out, pivot on
their admiration for the rock band Lynard Skynard, most of
whom died when their plane crashed in 1978. Actually, there is
nothing in this admiration, nor in the basic image they
stereotypically project that would make the Freebirds villains,
although they generally wrestle as such. No doubt, their
villainy is determined by the ageless conflict of the
generations, for they are decidedly a product of the modern
generation. They dress and act in such a way as to conjure up in
the minds of the conservative audience images of drugs, orgies
and other manifestations of the devient behaviour of the
young. The Freebirds do, of course, cultivate this image.
Michael Hayes, the evil genius of the Freebirds, particularly
motivates this response in the audience by his constantly
pointing out that he, better than anybody, can be "nasty" in
the ring. The word itself suggests the lifestyle of the punk
rocker with his sado/masochistic manner as initiated by Sid
Vicious and the Sex Pistols.

To really understand the Freebirds as villains, however,
one must also see their lifestyle in conflict with one that the
audience respects. This conflict of course initiated the birth of
the Freebirds when in New Orleans Michael Hayes dealt with
the threat of the audience favorite the Junkyard Dog by
blinding this massive man with some foreign substance that
he brought to the ring. This act in and of itself, because it so
clearly violates the rules of the game, would have made Hayes
and the Freebirds distinct villains. Moreover, the Junkyard
Dog would appear on television during his "recuperation" from
the lasting effects of the attack and point out that Hayes had
taken him from the role of provider and that as a result his
family was suffering. In other words, Hayes' act had attacked
the foundation of the family, the basis of American culture. His
evil was thus manifested, and the drama became complex,
except in the minds of the audience who clearly understood
what had happened and knew the appropriate response. They
developed a keen hatred for Hayes as letters to the promotion
clearly indicated. Just as the rock generation has questioned
the value of the traditional family and attacked this

sociological phenomon at its roots, so too had Hayes undermined the family stability of the Junkyard Dog and his wife and children. At the same time, Hayes was squandering his own talents and money living a life of frivolity, achieving nothing lasting, nothing permanent. To extend his sins, Hayes attracted a whole group of youthful admirers who wanted his lifestyle and saw his actions as justified in the pursuit of money and fame, both of which came from Hayes' defeating the Junkyard Dog.

Another significant wrestling villain, although one that is difficult to describe in a precise category, is the bully. He doesn't wear a distinguishing robe, nor does he speak with a strange accent. The actions of this villain are also the actions of other villains. Therefore, in a sense this villain has no group, but then his is the largest group of villains to review. He is in fact, despite the lack of distinguishing dress, the most easily recognized villain of all, for we all grew up with him living next door or just across the street.

Money has not made this villain evil nor has his nationality. He isn't a member of the lost generation. What makes him mean we do not know, but he is mean. He taunts his opponents, just as the neighborhood bully used to taunt the sissy kid who was always right and who always made good grades. He constantly tries to humiliate a good guy, just as the bully always used to throw a weak child in the mud just as the school bus arrived. He is mean just for pure meanness, and he loves professional wrestling, for he can make a living doing what he likes to do, hurt people. In other words, the bully is a perfect villain, for he is a part of every person's life, a legacy from the past. We know him from Charles Dickens to the Mr. Atlas ads in the commic books.

The wrestler who immediately comes to mind when we think of the bully in wrestling is Killer Karl Kox, a vicious truck driver looking man who proudly wears his KKK initials on the back of his wrestling trunks. Almost always, Kox appears when he is not wrestling in jeans and an old hat. When he wrestles, the audience sees that he has no athletic ability. The only holds he knows are a haymaker right hand and a kick to the groin. All he ever says during his interviews is that he wants to hurt someone, that he does not care about money or championships. He simply wants to hurt people. Thus, Karl has established himself as a genuine affront to the integrity of the sport.

In all of wrestling there are no greater villains than Ole and Gene Anderson. For the last twenty years they, referred to as the Minnesota Wrecking Crew, have rampaged their way through wrestlers and held the World's Championship Tag Team Belts. To really see the evil of these men and their nature as bullies, one must realize that they, like Karl Kox, care nothing about money. They are in the business to hurt people. Whom they hurt is insignificant. In fact, one of the great episodes of the wrestling promotion script occurred only about three years ago and involved the Anderson brothers. Ole had agreed to wrestle as the partner for his old nemesis Dusty Rhodes against the Masked Assasins. Both teams picked special referees. As it turned out the ring was filled with five villains and Rhodes, the ideal hero, although for this match the odds were supposedly even. Almost before the match began, however, all five villains attacked Rhodes and were beating him senseless when the third of the Andersons, Lars, jumped into the ring, supposedly to help administer pain. Surprisingly, he tried to pull his brothers out of the fight. They promptly turned on him and beat their own brother. Certainly this is sibling rivalry carried to the point that only a bully can take it.

The effectiveness of a Karl Kox or an Ole Anderson should be obvious. The psychological relief the fans feel at wrestling is finally seeing an old nemesis symbolically beaten by a good guy. Nowhere is this more true than when a bully gets what he deserves from some sort of hero, the hero who never came along when we were children to save us from mean kids. Thus, while perhaps the most difficult of wrestling villains to talk about in terms of distinguishing symbolic characteristics, the bully is by far the most effective at generating hostility from the audience and thus the most effective in the overall script of the sport. In fact, the only rival for audience hatred the bully has is the final class of villains, the manager.

Although not wrestlers themselves, managers are an integral part of the drama of professional wrestling and probably the most hated villains written into the script. Many have been previously discussed as they often fall within one of the other categories of villains such as the evil foreigner represented by the Great Mephisto and Michael Hayes of the punk rock generation. The point I want to make here is one about why managers are so hated. To see this clearly, we have to go back to the original of the wrestling managers, Homer Odell, whose memory stands bright in the minds of wrestling fans who have followed the sport for more than fifteen years.

Explaining why managers are always villains and why they are so hated by the fans is actually quite simple. When a manager is sitting outside the ring, one can be sure that there will be no fair fight before the match is through. Managers always get involved in the action, just enough to make sure that the villains they manage will win, but never, unless something goes wrong, enough to risk their own safety. They never enter a ring if the hero is on his feet or if he is facing them. When they do enter the ring, it is generally to bring in some weapon that they or their wrestlers will use to win a match. In essence they enjoy the fruits of the sport without taking the risks. They are, in other words, leeches who live off the blood and sweat of others. They are, therefore, contemptible creatures.

The prototype manager of the wrestling profession was Homer Odell. Throughout the 1960s, Odell managed the villainous team of Bronco Lubich and Aldo Bogni, both evil foreigners. He appeared at all their matches wearing a tuxedo and carrying a fancy cane, which he often used against his team's opponents when the referee was conveniently sending one of the good guys back to his own corner and preventing his rescuing his partner. Even this would not have made Odell such a villain except that anytime he appeared to be in danger, he would run rather than take his much deserved licking. We remember distinctly a match between Odell's men and the equally vicious Brute Bernard and Skull Murphy. The action got out of hand when the referee was injured, and Homer entered the ring where he broke his cane over Skull's bald pate. Amazingly, Skull was unhurt and prepared to give Odell his lesson, something that the fans had long wanted to see. (Skull had become a hero.) However, Odell quickly threw one of his men in the way and ran from the ring. Had he stood and fought, he could have been the hero. The fans were more than willing to see him beat on Skull Murphy. Unfortunately, Homer ran and tarnished what little respect any fan might have had for him. Homer has long since fallen out of sight, but a host of managers have taken his place, including Gary Hart who also wears a tuxedo and Freddie Blassie who carries a cane in the image of their creator.

An interesting side light to the manager villain is that probably the best script in wrestling revolves around a manager's wrestler turning his back on the man who has guided his career. It is a script replayed so often that fans now expect it and look for those first seeds of dissension that will finally spell doom for a manager. Boris Malenko has played the act throughout his career, nowhere better than in Florida a number of years ago where he brought onto the scene a monster of a man who had the personality of a robot. We never knew his name as Malenko spoke of him. Malenko put the man through a long series of gruelling matches with the very best competition the heroes in the area could offer. His man never lost or even looked close to losing. Finally, however, this was not good enough. Malenko wanted to see his past foes injured and would insult and slap his wrestler when he simply defeated them. Finally, in a rare television special, we saw the robot man turn on Malenko and absolutely devastate him. The fans, at this point, had a real hero to cheer for, a man who was not only good but who also had the strength generally reserved for villains. Unfortunately, the wrestler disappeared, leaving the fans asking something akin to "who was that masked man."

The only consistent characteristic that one might assign to a villain is that he breaks the rules in some way, not simply the rules of wrestling, but the rules of life as well. He destroys the order and must atone. Almost any villain can quickly become a hero if he simply takes as his opponent one more evil than himself; generally this means fighting a manager or an evil foreigner. The wrestling fans are, after all, a forgiving bunch, happy to welcome a convert. Whatever else one might say, however, the one sure fact about wrestling villains is that without them there would be no professional wrestling. A night of the scientific stuff, no way !

TheWrestling Hero

While the villain in wrestling may be the more interesting and varied character, the hero is equally necessary to create the conflict, thus the dramatic tension, which is necessary to any form of theatre. In fact, while wrestling fans may quickly grow weary of the acrobatics of two "scientific" wrestlers such as heroes are supposed to be, neither are they willing to partake of a steady diet of seeing two villains slug it out in the middle of the ring. In such a match, there is not the meaning that comes when good combats evil. Their usual reaction to such a match is to size up the two combatants, determine their sins, and pick one to be the hero, at least for the evening. The audience's decision may be somewhat arbitrary, but that they look for a hero is indicative of the morality of the wrestling audience. They are not just looking for blood. A match between villains will give them that. Rather, their competitive spirit and morality demand that there be a hero. Where one does not exist, they will create one to embody the spirit of good.

One journalist writing about the world of wrestling has defined the hero as follows: "Most of them are trim and handsome young men in their twenties or early thirties, the sort that little boys want to grow up to be, and men want to have as friends, and women want to have, also."[3] This definition, however, is no longer adequate, if it ever was, to defining the hero in today's wrestling world. As stated earlier, most villains will eventually wrestle as heroes, and defining the hero as distinctly as does the above description ignores this fact. One simply cannot tell a hero by such stereotypical qualities. The good guy in today's wrestling drama is more like what Anthony Hopkins calls the "new hero" as that figure has evolved from the antihero tradition and filtered into modern society through *One Flew Over the Cookoo's Nest* and *Easy Rider*. His heroism derives more from his sense of independence and self-sufficiency, always in the background there being a sense of fair play however submerged it might be.[4]

Nor can we define a wrestling hero as one who simply

follows the rules. Few good guys do so, although they do insist that their departures from those rules are required as they must "fight fire with fire." About the only generalization we can use to refer to the wrestling hero is that he must embody some significant virtue—patriotism, ethnic loyalty, love of family— a virtue that would allow him to follow the rules but that also gives him the determination and courage to battle the awesome wickedness of a villain on that villain's own terms. When such a virtue emerges from the inner depths of a villain, a hero is born. The following extended example will illustrate not only the conversion of a villain, but in so doing also point up the nature of a hero.

In 1980, Roddy Piper appeared rather dramatically on the wrestling scene in the Carolinas. Quickly he became a villain of some magnitude as he employed all manner of underhanded tactics to defeat his opponents. Piper even presented something of the evil foreigner image as he wore his Scottish kilt to the ring and played bagpipes before his matches. Finally, he hired a stable of bounty hunters such as Abdullah the Butcher and The Magnificent Murraco to do his dirty work. Piper's reign of terror lasted for two years and began to spread about the country before coming to an abrupt end.

In June 1982 Piper was attacked by a fan and sustained a knife wound in the chest. The story was covered in the press, but was then transformed by the wrestling commentators. The fans were told that Piper sustained his wound in the parking lot after the matches as he threw himself between a brawling bully and several children whom he was threatening with his knife. Piper's wound had been inflicted as he defended the same fans who had no doubt booed him earlier that same evening.

Wrestling fans were amazed. Asking themselves was there something good in Roddy Piper, they soon found their answer in what appeared to be a slight change in his ring behaviour and even in his attitude during television interviews. The drama finally played itself out as on television one of his hired assassins, Don Murraco, suddenly attacked the commentator Gordon Solie. Seeing Solie hurt, Piper unleashed his Scottish fury on Murraco. In the weeks that followed he, like Achilles avenging Patroklas, slaughtered villain after villain.

Traditional heroes did not quickly come to his side, as is usually the case in the reformed villain scenario, but because they did not the audience saw manifested that virtue in Piper, his willingness to stand alone, that had made him a hero or at least given him hero potential. In the arenas the fans chanted his name throughout his matches in a chorus that was reminiscent of the chants one heard during the 1980 winter Olympics as the American hockey team defeated the Russians.

The story of Roddy Piper illustrates one unquestionable fact about the wrestling hero. One act of courage can turn a wicked villain into a beloved hero, especially when that act of courage manifests an inherent virtue. Piper obviously had strong feelings about people, else he would not have worried about the children he saved or the safety of Gordon Solie. Moreover, he was willing to stand alone against whatever challenges he faced. Because a single virtue makes a hero, moreover, we can label, as we did with the villains, types of heroes depending upon that specific virtue which they embody.

Throughout the last half of the twentieth century, American culture has developed an increasing awareness of the South through the fiction of William Faulkner and Robert Penn Warren among others. Generally, however, the South has been seen as backward and intellectually, indeed morally, devoid of sophistication. The Jimmy Carter presidency changed that because, whatever else one might say, Carter was always regarded as a good man, if not a good President. The rest of the country began to Romanticize the South—much as Southerners have been doing since the Civil War—to such an extent that Billy Carter became something of a folk hero. This shift of attitude spawned one of the most successful wrestling heroes, the "good ol' boy," who displays some of that old fashioned Southern ethic that even a Yankee can appreciate.

Long before the Carter years, there had been heroes of the Southern wrestling circuit; the Kentuckians, who were a massive tag team, and Haystacks Calhoun, 600 hundred pounds of fury, were constant top bills. The appeal of these wrestlers, however, was more that of the carnival sideshow freak. No one considered them athletes even though they rarely lost a match. The new Southener in the wrestling ring is something different.

Southerners have taken pride—the pride of the defeated—since the Civil War for having fought the gallant fight. Theirs was, moreover, a fight for ideals. Thus in defeat, they were able to rise up with a sense of satisfaction that they did not lose the moral victory. Thus, the Southern hero in wrestling is a proud confederate type, proud of his heritage and proud of his ability in the ring. This virtue of pride may be simple, but it is one that has sustained him as a ring warrior, especially in the eyes of the fans. Perhaps more than any other type of hero, the "good ol' boy" takes a constant beating from his villain opponents because his pride tends to prevent him from engaging in tactics that go against the rules of the sport. This fact may endear him to the fans, but such pride also seems to get in the way. The resolution to a feud between such a hero and a villain, however, also follows from pride, pride of family.

A common stereotype of Southerners is that they are acutely devoted to their families. For a Southern boy hero, however, family loyalty is the vehicle for his success against villains. When he becomes involved in a ring war, suddenly he will find himself surrounded by cousins, brothers, even fathers, who join the feud, as with the Hatfields and McCoys, and see to it that the villain gets his just punishment. Afterall, nothing gets a Southern boy's blood boiling like seeing his family hurt.

Just such a drama kept the Southeastern promotion in an uproar for several months in 1983. For many years, the Fuller family has been the mainstay of that wrestling franchise. Ron Fuller, better known as the Tennessee Stud, is a constant contender for the World's Championship. Finally, he appeared to have captured that crown in Mobile, Alabama as he had Rick Flair in the dreaded Fuller leg lock when suddenly Bob Armstrong, the special referee for the match, turned on Fuller and helped Flair win the match. In so doing, he injured Fuller so that he was supposedly out of the wrestling business. Even worse, he and Fuller had long been wrestling partners. By turning on his friend and fellow Southerner to help the Northern Flair, Armstrong cast himself in the role of a Scallywag such as helped Carpetbaggers take over the South during Reconstruction. Armstrong, however, would be made to pay the price of such treachery. The very next week Robert Fuller, Ron's younger brother, appeared on television and began the task of avenging his brother. He, however, was no match for Armstrong's villainy. As stated earlier, Robert just could not sink to the low tactics of Armstrong. After his failure, Jimmy Golden, cousin to the Fullers, took up the task of revenge and suffered a similar fate. Armstrong appeared to have won. Evil reigned. In the months that followed the villainy of Armstrong went unchecked until suddenly Ron Fuller returned, his injury having healed so that he could in fact wrestle. In a desperate effort, Fuller attacked Armstrong at every turn until the two met in a Southern street fight, a no-holds barred type of match in which there is no referee to check the action. At last, Ron Fuller decisively defeated Armstrong and brought to a close a drama that had filled arenas throughout Alabama and Tennessee for months. In the denouement, the fans saw clearly two things. First, no evil is too great to conquer, even though it took three Fullers to do it. Most important, the audience saw that the family pride is a virtue that demands respect. Maybe Ron Fuller had to return to get the job done, but at least Robert and Jimmy Golden were willing to go after revenge. The moral is there far too clearly to demand further discussion.

The wrestling drama enacts the above script often. Nowhere does it work better than in the South with a "good ol' boy" hero who has developed a fan following based on his pride and his family loyalty. After-all, the drama is one that allegorizes the Southern experience in terms that the Southern audience can best appreciate.

One of the most rewarding products of the study of the popular arts is the ability to identify various manifestations of cultural myths that are in large part responsible for the shared moral ethic of a society. Our study of professional wrestling is, therefore, enhanced when, if possible, we can identify icons of popular culture that the wrestling drama shares with its fellow popular art forms. The masked avenger hero is just such a shared element, for he is a character drawn completely from the myth of the Lone Ranger. Like the masked lawman who arrived to rescue decent folk being threatened by some vile villain, the masked avenger in wrestling of the past twenty years has appeared suddenly on the scene just when a menacing villain or villains seemed completely to rule the ring world. After good has been restored, this valiant hero can just as quickly vanish. Also like the Lone Ranger, the masked wrestling hero is often mistaken for a bad guy as the mask in wrestling, like that of the rustler's bandana, often covers the face of a villain.

The masked avenger in wrestling is a special hero, for he embodies a spirit of mystery. The audience does not know who he is or where he comes from. A feeling of relief and wonderment occurs, therefore, when his mission—to defeat evil—becomes apparent. He is like an unexpected inheritance or a prolonged run of good fortune.

Mr. Wrestling I and his successor Mr. Wrestling II are the prototype of the masked avenger. Their very names and white masks suggest that they embody the ideals of competition and decency. Because they have no identity, they are pure virtue coming forth to administer justice. As a result they are wrestlers constantly faced with protecting their masks as if losing the mask will somehow strip them of their special powers, the way a comic book hero would be left defenseless without his cape.

Perhaps the greatest of all masked avengers was the Gladiator whose appearance was short lived but especially effective. His was a performance that very likely could not last long so beautifully was it rendered. The Gladiator appeared in Florida in the late 1960s when Boris Malenko, previously mentioned in this book, ruled the wrestling circuit. Malenko was for many years the epitome of evil. He had earned his reputation in the early sixties during the Cuban Missile Crisis by projecting the image of the Russian bully. Nowhere did his scam work more effectively than in Florida with its large Cuban population. Malenko had assembled a large stable of villains to do his dirty work and had eliminated all the local heroes. Suddenly the masked Gladiator appeared on television to defeat one of Malenko's men. No one had ever heard of him,. He became an instant hero, however, for he mustered the only recent challenge to Malenko. The next week he appeared again, once more to face one of Malenko's men, and repeated his earlier feat.

Malenko, of course, gathered all his forces. Yet every dirty trick failed. With wrestling prowess and equal skill in

deception, the Galdiator defeated his adversary. Malenko's
men deserted him until finally he was forced to enter the ring
himself. At that point, the Gladiator sought out the cause of the
plague and defeated the master-mind himself.

There is genuine romance in the saga of the masked
Gladiator. After finishing Malenko he disappeared. New
villains replaced Malenko as the old balance between good and
evil established itself once more. However, for the Florida
wrestling fan, there is always hope. No matter how great the
evil of the villains, the Gladiator is still out there, possibly
waiting until he is once more needed to restore good.

The point has been previously made that the dramatic
technique employed in the theatre of professional wrestling is
much like that of the morality play. To be more specific, the
professional wrestling scenario follows in the line of dramatic
literature that has evolved from the basic formula of
Prudentius' fifth century heroic poem *Psychomachia*. One
element of this formula is that as the characters who embody
the various vices and virtues meet in combat, they must be
somehow appropriately aligned. If gluttony is a vice, then he
must combat sobriety. Thus, if there is an evil foreigner in the
wrestling script, he must have a devoted American patriot to
offset him in the ring wars. In point of fact he does. The patriot
figure is one of the most successful wrestling heroes. To
understand his popularity, we need to review one other point
previously made about the wrestling drama.

Wrestling is a popular art, distinguishable from the
intellectual arts, because its appeal is to the audience's
emotions rather than to their minds. Patriotism, particularly
blind patriotism such as is manifested in the "my country right
or wrong" mind set, is an emotional way of responding to the
complexities of international life. It is the attitude of the Archie
Bunker person who loves Nixon but thinks his middle initial is
E. (We might note that Archie was a midget wrestling devotee.)
Therefore, the wrestling audience which looks for emotionality
in its artistic expression would find great delight in the
excessive patriotism of a ring hero. He is, moreover, the only
truly fit character to take on the goose stepping Nazis and
underhanded Japanese who fill the ring. Also worth noting is
that a sudden patriotic impulse has made instant heroes of

such ruthless villains as Ole Anderson and Stan Hanson. Whatever these bad guys may not share with the wrestling audience, they do have a common nationality.

Actually, sport and nationality are integrally related because of the impact of the Olympic Games. Most Americans feel a genuine sense of pride when they remember the emotional spectacle of the 1980 Olympic hockey team and its victory over the supposedly superior Russians. This point is particularly poignant when we consider that hockey is not a major spectator sport for most of the country. That, however, did not stop Southerners who know nothing of the sport from rejoicing at that team's victory. The chant of "U.S.A., U.S.A...." that filled the arena was enough to enlist a deep felt response, again because of the intensity of American patriotism. This same intensity of emotion can be felt in the wrestling arena when there is a bout between the Boston Battler Kevin Sullivan and Abdullah the Butcher, Paul Orndorff and Ivan Koloff or Dusty Rhodes and the Great Kabuki.

Having looked at the evil foreigner will help us come to grips with the precise nature of the patriot hero. He is, in fact, the mirror image of his villain counterpart. The evil foreigner scorns all rules; the patriot follows them. The evil foreigner has left his home to abuse the American system; the patriot has stayed at home to defend his sacred shores. The villain wrestles for money; the patriot for pride. The villain holds the fans in contempt; the patriot in esteem. Ultimately, however, we must remember that Americans pride themselves on their rugged pioneer spirit. Therefore, the patriot will break all rules, take any liberties that are necessary to defeat an evil foreigner and still be working within his proper realm of morality.

Ultimately, the conflict between a patriot hero and an evil foreigner becomes symbolic of traditional conflicts in American history. Thus, in each conflict a somewhat different hero type will evolve. The basics mentioned above will remain, but their manifestation will differ according to the precise conflict in which the hero is involved.

A previous discussion dealt with the conflict between Blackjack Mulligan and the Iron Sheik and how that conflict, occurring during the Iranian hostage crisis, allegorized for the audience their own sense of frustration and provided an outlet for such feelings. Mulligan took several beatings but endured like a patriot whose integrity gave him the strength he needed to continue his fight, just as Americans needed the strength to endure the long wait they faced until the hostages were released. In other words, during the hostage crisis the virtue of Americans was patience and resolve to continue. In his battle with an Iranian, Mulligan needed the same strengths. Therefore, his patriotic ethic was established by the conflict in which he was involved.

A second ring drama that comes to mind is that which emerged between Mr. Saito, a sneaky Japanese, and the former Marine Bob Armstrong. An Olympian and superior talent, Saito had issued challenges to all opponents, saying that he would pay $5000 to any man who could defeat him. He was first met by a series of supposed "men off the street" whom he defeated in quick order, often within a minute and always with a viciousness that left several injured. Throughout these episodes, the commentator blatantly used the term "Pearl Harbored" to refer to Saito's tactics, thus setting the frame of reference the audience needed to comprehend the symbolic nature of the drama. Saito's fallen victims became symbols for the American youth who were killed on December 7, 1941. Saito, like the Japanese army during the first two years of the war, appeared unstoppable, adding even a tremendous victory over Mr. Wrestling II to his list of conquests.

Suddenly there appeared on the scene Bob Armstrong whose son had been one of Saito's victims. Armstrong threatened Saito with a "good ole Georgia jaw jackin'" which he quickly delivered, over and over again. Like John Wayne, Armstrong spoke with assurance, employing all manner of patriotic cliches in his speeches. He was, however, able to fulfill his claims and to end the reign of terror of the Japanese tyrant. Armstrong was like the parents of those youth killed at Pearl Harbor who set out to avenge their children. This sense of family, thus patriotic, obligation became his mark of virtue. The revenge ethic is, after all, a moral stance that has been part of some of the most significant cultures in western civilization, including the Greek and British.

Not all the wrestling dramas between patriot heroes and

evil foreigners are so temporarily current; often they emerge
from the historical perspective. Even so, they are rooted in the
American psyche; therefore, the patriot hero is immediately
recognizable. An excellent example of the script revolving
around a historical conflict is that which placed Johnny
Weaver, a long standing hero, against the British Lord Alfred
Hayes. Both were retired wrestlers doing color commentary for
wrestling programs in the Carolinas, Weaver in his broken,
American, middle-class speech and Hayes with his eloquent
Oxford English rhetoric. The language patterns, however,
were only the outward manifestations of the differences
between the two. Hayes began condescending to Weaver and
referring to him as a mere commoner. He took on the *persona*
of the English aristocrat. In so doing, Hayes conjured up old
images of the pre-Revolutionary War period. Thus, Weaver
became the American pioneer. Maybe he did not speak "good
English," but everyone knew he could fight. The battle of
words, as one would expect, errupted into violence as Weaver
finally disassembled Hayes on television. His ethical frame-of-
reference was clear. He was determined that he was as good as
anyone else, no matter how poorly he was educated. He was,
moreover, unwilling to see the foreigner take a "high and
mighty" attitude about those persons who were his hosts. The
primitive democratic principle working here may not be
eloquent, yet it is about as sophisticated as that advocated by
the American colonists who fought in the Revolutionary War
and who, unlike Jefferson and the other members of the
Continental Congress, drew the political lines on the
battlefield, not in the documents exchanged between England
and the Colonies. In other words, Weaver became a founding
father image for the fans. His anti-intellectualism was in fact
quite in line with the basic American ethic that allows an
Alabama governor to refer to "pointed-headed intellectuals"
and still make a successful effort to sway the voting American
public. A final word here is that Lord Hayes found two Russian
wrestlers to seek revenge against Weaver and added a new
chapter to the Revolutionary War script, one that had
overtones of modern international conflict.

Perhaps one of the least noticed effects of the civil rights
movement of the 1950s and 1960s is that in 1982, quite unlike

or t

1962, a member of a minority group can step into the wrestling ring as a villain. Twenty years ago a Black man such as Sonny King would have been in serious trouble had he, as King did in 1982, entered the Georgia area and defeated with illegal tactics all the "good ol' " white boys in the area. However, the early days of wrestling set the trend, and now the hero from the minority groups is a well established character type. This is especially true in areas with large populations of minorites who contribute significantly to the gate receipts. In the South, Blacks are the primary hero type; in the New York area, Italians; and in the Southwest, Indians and Hispanics rule the ring. Having these minority hero figures may no longer be necessary to prevent trouble; now it is simply sound business. These wrestlers become symbols of those persons who have fought and will continue to fight to get to the top. Perhaps it is a too common generalization in our society that sports is one way out of the ghetto; however, in wrestling the generalization prepares an excellent foundation for drama. When the audience sees a minority hero fall victim to a villain, they can expect to see that hero call upon his racial or ethnic pride as his strengthening virtue. He can take his stand by saying that his people have come too far up the ladder of success to let a bullying wrestler stop his literal and their symbolic climb. Not only does this make such a hero a fitting figure of admiration for others from his racial or ethnic group, but also, because he has appealed to his roots, becomes a hero figure for others who can appreciate the virtue of pride in heritage in a general sense. Moreover, Black wrestlers, for example, do not side with other Blacks at all costs. In fact one of the most successful scripts in the wrestling drama is for one Black wrestler to oppose another. The villain will call his opponent an "Uncle Tom." The hero will respond that he treats people as people and that color is not the only factor to be considered. Similar dramas take place between members of other ethnic groups. In these scripts, however, the heroic virtue remains the same. A minority hero will always be a person proud of his heritage and determined to earn the respect of his people as well as all decent people in the wrestling audience. The final result is that wrestling legends such as Brunno Samartino, Tony Atlas, Mil Mascaras, and Pedro Morales fill the minds of a true wrestling enthusiast.

The out-of-the-ring career of Tony Atlas demands brief comment here. For years Atlas was a popular wrestling hero in the Georgia area. During the crisis in Atlanta that left thirty-two children murdered, Atlas took up a sort of crusade warning families about tending to their youngsters. His image as a hero allowed him to have an impact as parents and children of Atlanta's Black community suffered through the horror of that period. Had Atlas been a wrestling villain, one can only wonder whether he could have been a positive influence.

We have previously discussed the story of Leroy Brown; however, a further episode in his career will illustrate the effectiveness of the minority hero in the wrestling ring. His is a particularly fitting story as he has made effective use of the rise from the ghetto motif that is common to the scripts involving minority heroes.

An ever present chapter in the wrestling drama is for a part of the wrestling network to find itself flooded with villains who first capture all the regional titles and then dominate the area with their villainy as they keep those titles from the heroes who seek them. Next appears a new hero who promises to restore order rather than seek titles himself. Such was the situation in the Carolinas when Leroy Brown made his first appearance there. The good guys in the area had been overcome by an evil conspiracy that included the Anderson brothers, Sergeant Slaughter and his privates, and Roddy Piper, then a bad guy of the first order. Leroy, however, promised to guard the backs of the heroes as they fought this villainy. Everyone knew that in a fair fight the heroes could win. Whenever a villain received help from outside of the ring or decided to bend the rules, Brown, a three hundred pound Black man in overalls and a hard hat, would charge the ring and put things right.

Brown became an instant success with the fans. In the weeks that followed they learned that Leroy had grown up in Chicago's Southside and learned to fight on the streets where survival was tough. He never claimed to be a wrestler, just a brawler who would use his tactics to undo local bullies. Outside of the ring he was a gentle giant who always stopped at ringside before a match to talk with children and demonstrate his softer side. On the surface, there appears to be no ethnic bent to the story of Leroy Brown. Yet, in his struggle from the ghetto to the center arena of wrestling, he, it seemed, had held onto basic beliefs. He was strong but kind, always fair, and apparently incorruptible. But such is not the way of the wrestling champion.

Leroy finally became a villain after being humiliated by Rick Flair, the World's Champion. He found a manager and put on lavish wrestling tights to replace his ragged clothing. He began doing interviews wearing expensive suits and even more expensive jewelry. He was always talking money. But most important he stated his ambition to be the first Black World's Champion. He forgot his roots but talked of his heritage. This leads us to the final point. A minority member can be a hero only as long as he can be a hero for all the people. The moment he too distinctly emphasizes his ethnic background he can not have widespread appeal. He must be Black only to an extent that being Black means being something that all the fans can admire. When he takes up the image of an African or a flashy city type such as exploitation films depict, he must assume the villain's role. In other words the virtue of a wrestling hero must be a universal source of moral strength. The moment a wrestler identifies his role too specifically he risks losing his appeal to the majority of the fans which he needs to be seen as a hero.

Despite the general ridicule of professional wrestlers as pretend athletes, many grapplers have impressive credentials in the "legitimate" sporting world. Bob Roop, Ken Patera, and the Iron Sheik were Olympic wrestlers; Jack and Jerry Brisco were collegiate champions; Ernie Ladd and Wahoo McDaniels were professional football players, and Tony Atlas has remained a body building champion. While these are perhaps notables, many of today's wrestlers boast similar success in college or professional sport, particularly if we include competitive martial arts. Not surprising, therefore, is the fact that the bread and butter wrestling hero is the sports star turned wrestler. Clean cut college boys are a constant reminder to the audience that maybe, just maybe, there is something to wrestling after all.

We must not, however, in acknowledging the existence of this hero type forget that the audience will not long endure a match between two "scientific" wrestlers. They may applaud

good sportsmanship and even marvel at the well timed
choreography of the wrestlers, but what they are constantly
looking for in such a match is for one of the wrestlers to go bad,
draw blood, and in so doing create a drama. Then, and only
then, can one of the two achieve real hero status, for only then
will he be wrestling a villain. In other words, genuine athletic
prowess is a virtue that creates a hero only when it is a prowess
used against a villain.

A very fine illustration of this hero type is Bob Roop.
Though now a villain most of the time, Bob entered the
professional wrestling business fresh from his success in the
1968 Olympic games. After the protests of the Black athletes at
those games, he was able to capitalize on the image of the all
American boy. For weeks, Gordon Solie, the Florida
commentator at that time, prepared the audience for Roop's
arrival by giving progress reports of his transition training.
When Roop finally appeared, he had taken the nickname Mr.
Treerific to represent the concerns of a local environmental
group. As well, he wore Olympic tights colored with the stars
and stripes of Old Glory. Together, these two ploys set him
apart as a solid example of American youth. In the days of the
Vietnam protests, he was reassurance to the fans that not all of
the young people in the country had turned to drugs and sex.
Combined with his good looks, all this created an ideal hero.
The only people who were not impressed were the numerous
villains in the area who promptly defeated Roop as he began at
the bottom of the wrestling ladder. Roop survived, however,
and kept his image as a hero for some time. He eventually won
championships and even posed a serious threat to the World's
Champion. Finally, Roop went bad. His decision was in reality
based on his discovery that playing the bad guy was much
more fun and infinitely more challenging than was being a
hero. His conversion, however, was excellent drama, for he
became the rich kid type who grows up to shoot a President or
become a **Moonie.** He turned his back on all that was good even
though he appeared to have everything going for him.
Nonetheless, the conversion has stuck, much to the
satisfaction of Roop and the wrestling promotion.

Singing Roop's praises would be easy as he is a very decent
person. In fact, his initial image as a hero is generally in

keeping with his private personality. In the ring he, therefore, captured the essence of good, not in an allegorical sense as do so many of the other heroes, but rather in a down to earth way. Perhaps the hero like Roop whose image of good is based upon his athletic ability is so effective because seeing him in the ring allows the audience to cling to that cherished, though always questioned, belief that it just might be real.

Throughout the discussion of villains and of heroes, we have dealt in generalizations which is at best, a limited method of approaching any discussion. The simplistic dramatic form of wrestling, however, allows generalizations about character development, indeed encourages it. One final generalizaton is in fact needed. Any villain can become a hero, and any hero a villain. This fact points up the essential meaning of the wrestling drama, that no good is uncorruptible and that any evil can be redeemed. This dialectic creates eternal possibilities for drama, possibilities that the wrestling audience experience in their own lives, that captures the imagination of the fans and keeps them returning to the arenas hoping to see the birth of a new hero and fearing the possible loss of an old one.

Notes

[1] Bob Roop, interviewed in Morristown, Tennessee, March 1979.

[2] Billie Wahlstrom and Caren Dening, "Chasing the Popular Arts Through the Critical Forest," *Journal of Popular Culture,* 13:3 (Winter 1980), p. 415.

[3] W.C. Martin, "Friday Night in the Coliseum," *Atlantic Monthly,* 229 (March 1972), 84-85.

[4] Anthony Hopkins, "Contemporary Heroism-Vitality in Defeat," in *Heroes of Popular Culture,* ed. by Ray B. Browne, Marshall Fishwick, and Michael T. Marsden (Bowling Green, Ohio: Bowling Green University Popular Press, 1972), pp. 113-114.

Chapter Five
Professional Wrestling:
An American Ritual

AND Jacob was left alone; and a man wrestled with him until the breaking of the day. When the man saw that he did not prevail against Jacob, he touched the hollow of his thigh; and Jacob's thigh was put out of the joint as he wrestled with him.

Genesis 32: 24-25

Whatever else anthropologists might debate, they tend to be in agreement concerning two very significant observations about ritual. First, every culture, from the most primitive to the most sophisticated, has some form of ritual, and, second, that in most cultures ritual often evolves as a means of dealing with crisis, be the ritual an elaborate ceremony for the burial of the dead, a dance to bring rain to drought stricken crops, or a drama depicting man's confrontation with the divine during which he exposes his moral frailty. Regarding the characteristics of activities that constitute ritual, however, anthropologists are much more diverse in their opinions, particularly regarding definition and method of ritual. For the purpose of this chapter, therefore, we will appeal in the description of ritual primarily to the distinctions and definitions made by Margaret Mead in her essay "Ritual and Social Crisis." Professor Mead's work has been instrumental **as we have attacked here a two-fold purpose: first to establish** that professional wrestling is in fact ritual and second that despite the somewhat archetypal nature of professional wrestling, it is ritual particularly American because it dramatizes characters and conflicts that are especially significant to contemporary American culture.

Whenever discussing ritual, one will inevitably use the term drama, for whatever else it is, ritual is a re-creation, not a creation, a symbolic act that is a mode to meaning, not meaning itself, succinctly, a metaphor. Professional wrestling, too, is more a drama than a sport. The actors are athletes, but it is ultimately not their athletic prowess that is significant; rather their dramatic talents are what make them successful. But just as all drama is not ritual, this fact alone does not qualify professional wrestling as ritual. A further distinction is needed and is suggested in the following observation by Professor Mead:

> For an act to be ritual, in human terms, therefore, one must be conscious that it is ritual, and yet, at the same time, one must not be too conscious, because if the consciousness is too explicit the blend between the past and the present is lost.[1]

The point is well made and put into the context of our present study means that there must be illusion to some extent if the patterns of meaning inherent in ritual are to be communicated, but also there must be consciousness, else the symbol will be confused with the reality. Applied to professional wrestling, the audience must always be aware that the drama is not real, that the punches are being pulled, that the wrestler is bleeding from a self-induced razor nick, not the blows of his opponent, but at the same time entertain a sense of reality that what is happening is real if his response is to be emotional and intense, not merely critical and objective. W. C. Martin's splendid article on professional wrestling well points up this quality in the wrestling audience:

> The lust for blood is not simply ghoulish, but a desire to witness the stigmata, the apparently irrefutable proof that what is seen is genuine. Wrestling fans freely acknowledge that much of the action is faked, that many punches are pulled, that the moisture that flies through the air after a blow is not sweat but spit, and that men blunt the full effect of stomping opponents by allowing the heel to hit the canvas before the ball of the foot slaps the conveniently outstretched arm. They not only acknowledge the illusion: they jeer when it is badly performed.... Still, they constantly try to convince themselves and each other that at least part of what they are seeing is real. When Thunderbolt Patterson throws Bobby Shane through the ropes onto the concrete, a woman shouts defiantly, "Was that real? Tell me that wasn't real!"[2]

Indeed, the ability of the audience to hypnotize themselves into belief that their hero is really being brutalized has occasionally led to attacks by spectators and even dangerous riots. In November 1957, in fact, a riot broke out in Madison Square Garden as a result of the wrestlers' violence, and sixty-seven police were required to clear the mob of 13,000 blood-crazed fans.

This all important discussion suggests, we believe, why professional wrestling, which combines sport and drama, is ritual while theatre and actual sport such as football are not. Theatre is never real; the audience is never confused, except on rare occasions, that what is occuring on stage is reality. Theatre is completely symbol, and whatever meaning theatre has derives from the effectiveness of the symbol in reflecting reality. Football, on the other hand, which has often been mistakenly referred to as ritual, is completely real. The competition is not choreographed; the winners are not predetermined. Football, is, therefore, as unlike a fertility dance or a wedding ceremony as a plot is unlike a simile. Wrestling, however, solidly lodged between actual sport and **actual theatre, violates neither principle; it is neither** completely real nor completely symbolic, and to be completely either would disqualify its being ritual.

This distinction becomes even more clear and even more valid when one considers the effects the three activities have on the audience. It has long been established that the proper approach to theatre is for the audience member to suspend disbelief while observing the drama. The sports fan, on the other hand, needs no such mental preparation, for his response need not be intellectual to be appropriate. The wrestling fan, however, responds in a way that somewhat synthesizes the two. Certainly he responds emotionally as does a sports fan. But he also responds in some sense intellectually as does a theatre goer. Both responses are possible because the wrestling fan suspends his emotional disbelief by freeing his emotions from the dictates of his intellect in order to be able to accept the drama as real, at least to enough of an extent to become involved in the drama himself. The emotional suspension of disbelief, moreover, allows the final aspect of ritual—the repetition of ceremony—to work. Professor Mead addresses this issue well:

> Changes inevitably upset one: throw one out of the semi-
> automatic type of behavior which is only partly conscious and
> they project the participant into too great a consciousness.[3]

In other words, the wrestling fan's intellect would not allow an
acceptance of the scam were not the state of suspended
emotional disbelief strengthened by the almost complete
absence of surprise in the wrestling script. The following
observation by Herbert Brean, although made of scoff at the
activity, points up how completely professional wrestling
adheres to this part of the formula for ritual:

> It is widely acknowledged that professional wrestling is the most
> dependable of all sports since it is pure and conscientious fakery
> and never doublecrosses its fans with a dull, genuine exhibition.[4]

As a result, therefore, wrestling evokes audience response as
intense as if it were real without being real; it walks a fine line
here, but because it walks this line, we are justified in calling it
ritual which we cannot do in reference to a performance of
Hamlet or the playing of the Super Bowl.

Ritual, however, must have meaning as well as method
which leads to the second proposition of this paper, that
professional wrestling is, in essence, the ritual of Americana.

Professor Mead establishes clearly that there is a definite
relationship between a society's periods of crisis and its rituals:
"Throughout human history man has employed ritual
behavior to deal with critical moments."[5] Aidan O. Dunleavy
and Andrew W. Miracle, Jr. make the same point when they
describe the five dimensions of ritual, one being that ritual is
both a cohesive activity which focuses a group's attention on a
shared concern and a second being that ritual "might funciton
as an adjustive response to stress or as a mechanism for coping
with anxiety."[6] Professional wrestling adheres to this quality
of ritual at two specific levels of meaning, archetypal and
stereotypical, to use the distinction established by Wahlstrom
and Demings in "Chasing the Popular Arts Through the
Critical Forest."[8] The archetypal are those cross culture
conflicts and patterns such as the conflict of good and evil that
are not unique to any culture. The stereotypical patterns of
meaning in the ritual of professional wrestling, those that

make it more specifically an American ritual and thus a cohesive force, are those that have in fact evolved out of the social crises of American culture and allow it to relieve stress. We can see this point more clearly by looking at two specifics, the characters that participate in the conflicts and the way those conflicts are settled, restated, the ethics of combat.

Because so much of our discussion has served to point up qualities of ritual of a more general nature, we would do well to first establish by quoting Professor Mead that ritual can legitimately appeal to a specific culture:

> I think this would be a useful distinction to keep in mind: ritual is concerned with relationships, either between a single individual and the supernatural, or among a group of individuals who share things together. There is something about the sharing and the expectation that makes it ritual.[8]

Thus, when we discuss the characters of professional wrestling, we must see them not just as villains and heroes but, and this is not difficult, as characters whose heroism and villainy conform to what Jung might call the collective American unconscious. Much the same can be said of the specific conflicts and the ethics of combat which are not just those of the forces of good versus the forces of evil, for these two forces combat in ways that, again, conform completely to American mores.

The characters of professional wrestling have already been discussed, but let us begin a short discussion by looking at the following observation by William Martin:

> The overwhelming majority of professional wrestling matches pit the Good, the Pure, and the True against the Bad, the Mean, and the Ugly, and a man with a flair for provoking anger and hatred has an assured future in the sport. Since shortly after World War II, the most dependable source of high displeasure has been the Foreign Menace, usually an unreconstructed Nazi or a wily Japanese who insults the memory of our boys in uniform with actions so contemptuous one cannot fail to be proud that our side won the war.[9]

The second part of Martin's statement is particularly significant. First, it points up how specifically the nature of the villains complies with what Americans hate most, the evil foreigner. Second, and more important, Martin shows how this aspect of the ritual would assist in society's dealing with current crises. For example, as we faced the Iranian crisis, professional wrestling responded with numerous matches pitting the flag waving American against the evil foreigner, turning what had been undertones into full fledged drama. More specifically, Kevin Sullivan, "The Boston Battler," nicknamed for the birth city of the American Revolution, recently destroyed after months of bloody conflict The Great Mephisto, Abdullah the Butcher, and Maniac Mark Lewin, an American corrupted by the foreign influence. Mr. USA, Tony Atlas, chased the German Baron von Raschke from the state of Georgia, and essentially every wrestler in the Carolinas has been after the Iron Sheik, an Iranian who constantly insults the American way of life. When the audience sees villains as these do their dirt, they are affirmed in their fear and hatred, but more, when a local hero finally defeats one of these villains, usually after a long and bloody feud that has filled the arenas for months, the fans are confirmed in their feelings of moral superiority based on the belief that "might is right."

There are, of course, many more types of villains, all equally repulsive to the American ethic: Killer Karl Kox who wears his KKK initials on his warm up robe, and who does occasionally appear in the South as a hero, Ole and Gene Anderson who betrayed their brother Lars, beating him bloody and violating the concept of family loyalty, Bob Roop and Ken Patera who were Olympic athletes, now fallen to rule breaking tactics, and the host of disciples of Gorgeous George whose narcissism soils the more of humility.

Generally less interesting and, therefore, much more easy to define are the heroes of professional wrestling whom Martin describes as "Clean-cut, Finely Muscled Young (men) who never fight(s) dirty until provoked beyond reason and who represent(s) the Last, Best, Black, Brown, Red, or White Hope for Truth, Justice, and the American Way."[10] This definition, however, reflects only one of the types of heroes, the college athletes, AAU champions, who come from good familes and who bring their fine upbringing into the ring with them by behaving as gentlemen. Jack Brisco is a representative example as he rose from college star to World Heavyweight Champion, showing that good could prevail. But such heroes are rare, for, afterall, they are boring when you get right down to it and are especially ineffective dramatically. Much more popular and for this study much more significant are those heroes who grew up on a small tenant farm or the streets of big cities, learned to fight to survive, and who despite all their hardships realized along the way that the only way to get ahead is to be strong enough to be good. Men with such a heroic ethic, reminders of the days of knights and chivalry in a sense, are the stuff out of which folk heroes are made in America because they, like Rocky, are a constant reminder that this is the land of opportunity where anyone can get ahead. The best example of such a hero is the plummer's son Dusty Rhodes, appropriately tagged "The American Dream." When not making BC headache powder commercials and telling us about pain, Dusty is travelling the country, no longer looking for the World's Championship, but rather confronting evil wherever it exists. His primary targets are Ole and Gene Anderson who Rhodes says are "tearin' apart the fabric of wrestlin'. They're anti-family and there can't be none of that in wrestlin'. Wrestlin' is a family sport, a place where you take your wife and kids to, where the old-fashioned principles of honor, integrity, and devotion are reared. Anyone threatnin' that threatens wrestlin' and threatens me."[11]

Not only do Rhodes' words sound like a statement from the moral majority, they also echo principles as American as, well, as wrestling. And although made in a publicity scam, his **words also suggest the second point we wish to make, that** wrestling demonstrates a set of ethics peculiarly American. Certainly the villains fight dirty, striking their opponents with foreign objects pulled from their trunks or ganging up on a good guy, two on one, three on one, four on one, whatever it takes to beat him senseless. Afterall, as Professor Hendricks points out, "the villains in these...matches must prove an adequate test for the heroes' moral courage, for in religious terms, if Satan is trivial, what is the power of the Christian who overcomes him?"[12] And, of course, the good guys are scientific wrestlers who resort to roughhouse tactics only as a last resort and only after being sufficiently motivated. The ethical framework of professional wrestling, however, is more complex than this and rests more specifically on two distinctly American values. First, Americans have traditionally cheered an underdog, and second, we will accept the conversion of the most ruthless villain if the conversion is properly motivated and genuinely enacted in the ring. We really don't care about tactics as long as the bad guys get beat and the good guys do the beating. Two specific examples will demonstrate.

Several years ago, the big Texan Stan Hanson was a ruthless bunkhouse brawler who ran roughshod over every local hero in the state of Georgia. Yet, all his sins were soon forgotten when Stan engaged in a ring feud with Abdullah the Butcher, a most vicious-foreign villain. During his battles, Stan's tactics remained exactly the same, but he, the American, was cheered because he had found an adversary who deserved his wrath. Before long, all the "good ol' boys" Stan had defeated were standing right beside him, their best friend. A second example was the Masked Superstar who reverted to hero status simply on the basis of his feud with Ray "The Crippler" Stevens, Jimmy Snuka, and Gene Anderson who "Pearl Harbored" him after a television match. The Superstar, like Stan, did not change his tactics at all; he simply used them to serve a moral end. Even more, he admitted that he was no different; his honesty won him friends, however, because it is a virtue greater than the evil of his tactics. All this translates into one simple principle: no matter what a person does, if he does it with a proper motivation and is honest about it, we Americans will applaud any destruction he then levels against a genuine lying, cheating, villain. Indeed, we enjoy this "unparalleled opportunity to indulge in aggressive and violent impulses."[13]

We want to conclude by returning to a point made in the introduction that ritual serves as a method for a society to deal with the social crises it faces. This particular quality applies to both the method and meaning of professional wrestling. In terms of method, professional wrestling really never changes. The villains are basically the same, as are the heroes; year after year and time after time, a hero is attacked by a villain; perhaps the bad guy interferes in a match and causes the good guy to lose a championship or injures him by using dirty tactics. The feud continues for weeks without resolution, both wrestlers appearing on televison threatening destruction, the villain constantly getting the upper hand because he fights dirty, or at least he fights dirtier than does the good guy.

Finally, in a cage match with no disqualification and with wrestlers stationed around the ring to throw back anyone who tries to run, the hero suffers a terrible beating but finally triumphs, usually. This repetition, however, is crucial to ritual, Professor Mead says:

> Only if ritual is conducted in the same way, only if the same words are spoken in the same order and accompanied by the same gestures, will the same feeling of security be present.[14]

Mead's comment is directly to the point, for in wrestling the audience knows basically what will happen; especially they know that the hero is going to take a beating:

> The Portrayal of Life that unfolds in the ring is no naive melodrama in which virtue always triumphs and cheaters never win. Whatever else these folks know, they know that life is tough and filled with conflict, hostility and frustration. For every man who presses toward the prize with pure heart and clean hands, a dozen Foreigners and so-called Intellectuals and Sons-of-bitches seek to bring him down with treachery and brute force and outright meanness.[15]

But what wrestling does as ritual that helps us through bad times is that it does prove that villains can be defeated, that heroes who embody good American ideals can win and that, whatever else, determination and dedication can and do triumph over deceit and treachery. And if nothing else of value can be found in professional wrestling, it does give us hope, hope that we can be greater than Russia, that Iran cannot push us too far, that the energy crisis can be licked, that America can survive whatever tests she faces—we know because we see it happen every Saturday night in some local high school gym, a National Guard Armory, or run down old civic center where we come together to witness what we know to be true and hope for what we know to be possible.

Notes

[1]Margaret Mead, "Ritual and Social Crisis," *The Roots of Ritual*, ed. James D. Shaughness (Grand Rapids, Michigan: William B. Erdman's Pulbishing Company, 1973), p. 92.

[2]W. C. Martin, "Friday Night in the Coliseum," *Atlantic Monthly,* 229 (March 1972), p. 87.

[3]Mead, p. 91.

[4]Herbert Brean, "Wrestling Script Gone Awry," *Life*, 43 (December 2, 1957), p. 165.

[5]Mead, p. 89.

[6]Aidan O. Dunleavy and Andrew W. Miracle, Jr., "Sport: An Experimental Setting for the Development of a Theory of Ritual," *Play as Context: 1979 Proceedings of the Association for the Anthropological Study of Play*, ed. Alyce T. Cheska (West Point, N.Y.: Leisure Press, 1981), p. 118.

[7]Billie Wahlstrom and Caren Deming, "Chasing the Popular Arts Through the Critical Forest," *Journal of Popular Culture*, 13:3 (Winter 1980), p. 415.

[8]Mead, p. 89.

[9]Martin, p. 83.

[10]*Ibid.*

[11]"The Greatest Bounty Hunters in History: Dusty & Andre Team to Destroy the Andersons," *The Wrestler*, January 1981, pp. 35 & 58.

[12]T. Hendricks, "Professional Wrestling as Moral Order," *Sociological Inquiry*, 44:3 (1974), 181.

[13]Martin, p. 86.

[14]Mead, p. 92.

[15]Martin, p. 87.

Index

166